Book F

Specific Skill Series

Locating the Answer

Richard A. Boning

Fifth Edition

SRA/McGraw-Hill

Columbus, Ohio

Cover, Back Cover, ZEFA/Germany/The Stock Market

SRA/McGraw-Hill

A Division of The **McGraw·Hill** *Companies*

Printed in the United States of America.

Send all inquiries to:
   SRA/McGraw-Hill
   8787 Orion Place
   Columbus, OH 43240-4027

ISBN 0-02-687956-5

   6 7 8 IPC 02 01 00

To the Teacher

PURPOSE:

As its title indicates, LOCATING THE ANSWER develops pupils' skill in finding *where* sought-for information can be found within a passage. Pupils must carefully read and understand each question, grasp phrase and sentence units, and discriminate between pertinent and irrelevant ideas.

FOR WHOM:

The skill of LOCATING THE ANSWER is developed through a series of books spanning ten levels (Picture, Preparatory, A, B, C, D, E, F, G, H). The Picture Level is for pupils who have not acquired a basic sight vocabulary. The Preparatory Level is for pupils who have a basic sight vocabulary but are not yet ready for the first-grade-level book. Books A through H are appropriate for pupils who can read on levels one through eight, respectively. **The use of the *Specific Skill Series Placement Test* is recommended to determine the appropriate level.**

THE NEW EDITION:

The fifth edition of the **Specific Skill Series** maintains the quality and focus that has distinguished this program for more than 25 years. A key element central to the program's success has been the unique nature of the reading selections. Nonfiction pieces about current topics have been designed to stimulate the interest of students, motivating them to use the comprehension strategies they have learned to further their reading. To keep this important aspect of the program intact, a percentage of the reading selections have been replaced in order to ensure the continued relevance of the subject material.

In addition, a significant percentage of the artwork in the program has been replaced to give the books a contemporary look. The cover photographs are designed to appeal to readers of all ages.

SESSIONS:

Short practice sessions are the most effective. It is desirable to have a practice session every day or every other day, using a few units each session.

To the Teacher

SCORING:

Pupils should record their answers on the reproducible worksheets. The worksheets make scoring easier and provide uniform records of the pupils' work. Using worksheets also avoids consuming the exercise books.

It is important for pupils to know how well they are doing. For this reason, units should be scored as soon as they have been completed. Then a discussion can be held in which pupils justify their choices. (The Integrated Language Activities, many of which are open-ended, do not lend themselves to an objective score; thus there are no answer keys for these pages.)

GENERAL INFORMATION ON *LOCATING THE ANSWER*:

At the earlier levels the answer to the question is worded much the same as the question itself. As the books increase in difficulty, there is less correspondence between the phrasing of the question and the phrasing of the answer.

SUGGESTED STEPS:

1. Pupils read the question *first* and then look for the answer.

2. Pupils use the range finder (sentence choices) in Books B–H. The letters or numbers in the range finder (below the question) indicate which sentences must be read to locate the answer to the question. In the Picture Level, the pupils decide which picture answers the question. For Preparatory and A levels, the number before the question tells the paragraph to read.

3. Pupils read the sentences with the question in mind. (On the Picture Level, pupils look at the pictures. On the Preparatory and A levels, pupils read the paragraph.)

4. When using Books B–H, pupils write (in the space on the worksheet) the letter or number of the sentence that answers the question. On the Picture Level, pupils write the letter of the correct picture choice. On the Preparatory and A levels, pupils write the letter of the correct word choice.

Additional information on using LOCATING THE ANSWER with pupils will be found in the **Specific Skill Series Teacher's Manual**.

RELATED MATERIALS:

Specific Skill Series Placement Tests, which enable the teacher to place pupils at their appropriate levels in each skill, are available for the Elementary (Pre-1–6) and Midway (4–8) grade levels.

About This Book

People read for different reasons. You may read a story just for fun. You may read a letter from a friend to find out what your friend has been doing. You may read a book or an article to find the answer to a question.

Reading to find information is different from other reading. You are reading with a particular purpose. This means that you have to know what you are looking for. You need to read with your questions in mind. You can think of this as searching for something you have lost. You don't know where the lost object is, but you know what you are looking for.

Knowing what you are looking for can help you decide where to look. You wouldn't look for a missing shoe in the refrigerator. You might look for it under your bed or in the closet. You wouldn't look for the answer to a question about whales in a paragraph about dolphins. You would try to find the answer in a paragraph about whales.

Knowing how to locate information is an important reading skill. For each unit in this book, you will find ten questions about a piece of writing. The answers to the questions appear in that piece of writing. Your job is to locate the answers. You do not actually answer the questions. Instead, you tell **where** to find the answers.

Read this paragraph. Which sentence answers the question "Who granted land in Pennsylvania to William Penn?"

> (**1**) William Penn came to Pennsylvania in 1682 as governor of the colony. (**2**) King Charles II had granted to him the lands of the Pennsylvania region. (**3**) Penn made a treaty with the Native American Indians there shortly after he arrived. (**4**) He paid the Indians for much of the land King Charles had given him, even though he did not need to do so.

The answer is in sentence (**2**).

As you work on each unit in this book, read the questions first. Look at the five numbers below each question. Then look for the answer in the sentences with those five numbers in the piece of writing. Read the sentences with the question in mind. Tell which sentence gives the answer.

UNIT 1
Crossroads of East and West

(1) At the eastern end of the Mediterranean Sea, where Europe meets Asia, lies a country containing a fascinating mixture of Western and Eastern ways of life. (2) Most of its people wear European clothing and have adopted Western ways of living, yet they follow the Muslim religion of the Middle East. (3) They speak an Asian language but use the European alphabet. (4) This country at the crossroads of East and West is Turkey.

(5) Turkey's location has given it a long and turbulent history. (6) It is shaped like a thumb of Asia reaching out into the Mediterranean and Black seas and touching the southeastern tip of Europe. (7) A small part of the nation, its thumbnail, is actually in Europe. (8) The European and Asian parts of Turkey are separated by a narrow body of water called, at the western end, the Dardanelles and, at the eastern end, the Bosporus. (9) Over the ages wars and threats of wars for control of these waters have frequently upset Turkish life. (10) In ancient times the Persians, the Greeks, and the Romans controlled much of Turkey. (11) From the 1300s to 1923 the land was known as the Ottoman Empire. (12) Then a republic was proclaimed, and modern reforms, such as giving rights to women, were begun. (13) Even today the old Turkish ways and the new sometimes clash.

(14) Even Turkey's geography reflects opposites. (15) The European parts, called Thrace, and the Asian coastal lowlands are fertile. (16) Most of the rest of the nation, called Anatolia, consists of mountains and high, dry plateaus. (17) Along the coasts the winters are mild and rainfall is abundant. (18) In the interior, however, winters can be bitter, with temperatures reaching forty degrees below zero Fahrenheit, and summers are dry and scorching.

(19) In the 1920s Turkey's new rulers began to change the country's economy from a mostly agricultural to a more varied one. (20) In 1923 the entire nation had only 118 factories. (21) Today there are thousands. (22) Industry has now surpassed agriculture in the amount of money it earns. (23) Yet nearly three out of five Turkish workers still toil on farms and in pastures. (24) Turkey is famous for the tobacco it grows and exports. (25) Large quantities of cereal grains, cotton, olives, and figs are grown also. (26) From Turkey's factories come processed foods and beverages, textiles, steel, fertilizers, and machines.

(27) Visitors to Turkey can experience a variety of sights. (28) In the mountains the poorest people roam the hills and valleys with their sheep or cattle and live in caves. (29) The cities are crowded with both the poor and those who are better off. (30) The chief cities are Ankara, the capital, and Istanbul, the largest metropolis. (31) Located on the European side of the Bosporus, Istanbul is one of the world's most historic cities. (32) It was formerly known as Byzantium and then Constantinople. (33) The city is famous for its beautiful mosques, or Muslim houses of worship, with their graceful domes and tall, slender towers. (34) Visitors can also enjoy two Turkish foods that have become popular in America —yogurt and shish kebab—while watching one of the Turks' favorite sports—greased wrestling.

UNIT 1
Crossroads of East and West

1. Do the Turkish people use an Asian or European alphabet?

   Sentence   **(1)**   **(2)**   **(3)**   **(4)**   **(5)**

2. What effect did Turkey's location have on its history?

   Sentence   **(4)**   **(5)**   **(6)**   **(7)**   **(8)**

3. Where are the Dardanelles located?

   Sentence   **(8)**   **(9)**   **(10)**   **(11)**   **(12)**

4. Do the old and new Turkish ways ever cause a conflict?

   Sentence   **(11)**   **(12)**   **(13)**   **(14)**   **(15)**

5. Is Anatolia described as a mountainous section?

   Sentence   **(15)**   **(16)**   **(17)**   **(18)**   **(19)**

6. How many factories operated in 1923?

   Sentence   **(18)**   **(19)**   **(20)**   **(21)**   **(22)**

7. Does Turkey use all the tobacco it grows?

   Sentence   **(22)**   **(23)**   **(24)**   **(25)**   **(26)**

8. Is there much of interest for visitors?

   Sentence   **(24)**   **(25)**   **(26)**   **(27)**   **(28)**

9. Are the cities inhabited by only poor people?

   Sentence   **(26)**   **(27)**   **(28)**   **(29)**   **(30)**

10. What are the two principal cities in Turkey?

    Sentence   **(30)**   **(31)**   **(32)**   **(33)**   **(34)**

UNIT 2
A Land of Beauty

(1) "Switzerland!" Visions of lofty mountains and country scenes accompany the word. (2) Thoughts of a tiny, landlocked nation, populated by industrious people, fill the mind's eye. (3) The impressions are accurate, yet they do not tell the full story of the people's attempts to master their beautiful environment.

(4) The presence of the mountains has a vast influence on the lives of those who live among them. (5) The rugged nature of the land has a direct influence on the occupations of the people. (6) Farming is, of necessity, somewhat limited. (7) Approximately one-third of the land is not fit for farming. (8) The nation's chief crop is potatoes. (9) Herds of goats and sheep are numerous. (10) Dairying is the chief agricultural industry. (11) Tending over one million dairy cows is a major task for the Swiss farmers. (12) Dairy products are the chief farm exports.

(13) With limited natural resources, the Swiss have had to turn their attention to the development of industries. (14) They have succeeded in manufacturing in spite of a lack of raw materials. (15) The Swiss specialize in goods of high quality that are sufficiently small in size so that shipping costs are kept low. (16) Watches, textiles, metalwork, shoes, and chemical products make up a major portion of Swiss exports.

(17) The Swiss have no language of their own. (18) They use the language of their neighbors. (19) The largest number of Swiss, sixty-five percent, speak German. (20) The second largest group, about eighteen percent, speak French. (21) About twelve percent speak Italian. (22) Most of the remainder speak an old language, Romansch. (23) In spite of their language differences, the Swiss get along remarkably well with each other, as indeed they do with people of other nations. (24) Switzerland has not been involved in a war for over 165 years.

(25) No country offers more spectacular scenery than Switzerland. (26) Glittering, snow-capped mountains tower over green valleys, sparkling lakes, and quaint villages that are the glory of the Swiss landscape. (27) So important is the tourist industry that almost five percent of the Swiss people work in the hotel and restaurant business—to cater to the wishes of the more than five million who visit the country each year. (28) Tourists visit Switzerland for sporting thrills as well as for its magnificent scenery.

(29) The Matterhorn, located on the Swiss-Italian border, is Switzerland's most famous mountain. (30) Teams of mountain climbers have attempted to scale its sides, almost fifteen thousand feet high, for many years. (31) Luxury hotels, skilled guides, ski lifts, skating rinks, and toboggan slides provide visitors to the area with every accommodation.

(32) Because Switzerland has long been removed from the bitter wars that have troubled neighboring lands, it has been a center for international organizations. (33) The International Red Cross, founded in Geneva in 1863, is the best known of these. (34) The Red Cross helps victims of wars and other disasters and keeps records of prisoners of war. (35) While keeping its own peace, Switzerland maintains an open door as a haven for war refugees.

UNIT 2
A Land of Beauty

1. What thoughts of Switzerland fill the mind's eye?
   Sentence   **(1)**   **(2)**   **(3)**   **(4)**   **(5)**

2. What percentage of the land is not fit for farming?
   Sentence   **(4)**   **(5)**   **(6)**   **(7)**   **(8)**

3. What is the nation's chief crop?
   Sentence   **(7)**   **(8)**   **(9)**   **(10)**   **(11)**

4. Why do the Swiss manufacture products that are small?
   Sentence   **(11)**   **(12)**   **(13)**   **(14)**   **(15)**

5. In what respect has Switzerland borrowed from nearby countries?
   Sentence   **(14)**   **(15)**   **(16)**   **(17)**   **(18)**

6. What percent of the Swiss speak German?
   Sentence   **(17)**   **(18)**   **(19)**   **(20)**   **(21)**

7. Do any Swiss speak Italian?
   Sentence   **(21)**   **(22)**   **(23)**   **(24)**   **(25)**

8. How many people visit Switzerland each year?
   Sentence   **(24)**   **(25)**   **(26)**   **(27)**   **(28)**

9. What are Switzerland's two major attractions?
   Sentence   **(27)**   **(28)**   **(29)**   **(30)**   **(31)**

10. Why has Switzerland been a center for international organizations?
    Sentence   **(31)**   **(32)**   **(33)**   **(34)**   **(35)**

UNIT 3
The World's Largest Lake

(1) The Russians and native people of Russia call Lake Baikal "the sacred lake." (2) It is the largest lake on Earth. (3) It covers 400 miles of the Siberian Plateau in Russia.

(4) Baikal is the deepest lake on the planet—5,750 feet of water and another four miles of sediment below that. (5) The water and sediment combined extend seven times deeper than the depth of the Grand Canyon. (6) The lake lies in a depression, or rift, in Earth's crust. (7) This was caused by the movement of two structural plates in Earth's surface. (8) These plates are still separating, so the rift will continue to grow and Baikal will get even deeper.

(9) Lake Baikal has about the same surface area as does Lake Superior. (10) Yet, because of its depth, it holds as much water as the five Great Lakes combined. (11) This is about one fifth of all the fresh water on Earth. (12) If the lake were to be drained, it would take more than a year for all the rivers and streams on Earth to refill it.

(13) Baikal is about twenty-five million years old. (14) This makes it the oldest lake on the planet. (15) Lake Tanganyika, in east-central Africa, is the second oldest—two million years. (16) By comparison the Great Lakes, which were gouged out of the earth by glaciers, filled with water about 15,000 years ago when the glaciers receded. (17) Tanganyika is also the second deepest lake—4,700 feet.

(18) Lake Baikal is a fascinating body of water for a number of reasons. (19) It has living ecosystems that extend to its bottom. (20) It is believed that oxygen circulates deep into the lake because of tides that are created by the pull of the sun and moon. (21) Such tides would not be present in shallower bodies of water. (22) Also, hot water vents exist at the bottom of Lake Baikal. (23) The moderate water temperature at that depth also contributes to the richness of life.

(24) Baikal has remained fairly clean over time. (25) One organism, the *epishura*, helps keep it crystal clear. (26) This tiny crustacean strains impurities from the water. (27) Many of the lake's animals and plants are native only to it, including the *nerpa*, the world's only freshwater seal.

(28) However, you should not think that Lake Baikal is untroubled. (29) As population and industry increase along its shores, pollution is taking its toll. (30) The Trans-Siberian Railway, built over a century ago, brought eroded soil into the lake. (31) Factory wastes and dams have also contributed to its degradation.

(32) People can no longer drink water straight from the lake. (33) Whitefish and other fish populations have begun to decline, affecting commercial fishing. (34) The *epishura* has lost seven percent of its habitat.

(35) Early Russian environmentalists were denounced for their activities. (36) Today the environmental movement is gaining strength. (37) One of its key goals is the protection of the Lake Baikal ecosystem.

UNIT 3
The World's Largest Lake

1. Is Lake Baikal larger than the Great Lakes?

   Sentence   (1)   (2)   (3)   (4)   (5)

2. Is Lake Baikal as deep as it will ever be?

   Sentence   (4)   (5)   (6)   (7)   (8)

3. To which lake is Baikal similar in terms of surface area?

   Sentence   (9)   (10)   (11)   (12)   (13)

4. Is Lake Baikal older or younger than Lake Tanganyika?

   Sentence   (14)   (15)   (16)   (17)   (18)

5. Do tides exist in shallow bodies of water?

   Sentence   (19)   (20)   (21)   (22)   (23)

6. What characteristic of Lake Baikal has remained much the same over time?

   Sentence   (24)   (25)   (26)   (27)   (28)

7. What is the organism called that helps keep Lake Baikal clear?

   Sentence   (25)   (26)   (27)   (28)   (29)

8. What is increasing population around Lake Baikal causing?

   Sentence   (29)   (30)   (31)   (32)   (33)

9. How have the fish in Lake Baikal been affected by pollution?

   Sentence   (33)   (34)   (35)   (36)   (37)

10. Is the Russian environmental movement today weakening?

    Sentence   (33)   (34)   (35)   (36)   (37)

UNIT 4
Land of Timber

(1) Finland is a nation born in hardship. (2) For six hundred years it served as a battleground for its two neighbors, Russia and Sweden. (3) During this time twelve major wars were fought on Finnish soil between these opponents. (4) In spite of this, the Finns emerged with an independent and prosperous state.

(5) Few nations have the rugged beauty that can be found in Finland. (6) Although it is a land of only 130,000 square miles—about half the size of Texas—it has more than sixty thousand lakes. (7) Its coast is long and rough. (8) More than two-thirds of the nation is carpeted with splendid forests of pine, spruce, and fir. (9) Yet few nations have had to struggle with elements as harsh.

(10) Many Finns are used to bitter arctic weather. (11) One-third of the nation lies north of the Arctic Circle. (12) Despite the bitter cold and long winters, Finland has become self-sufficient in agriculture. (13) Scientific farming has developed strains of wheat, rye, barley, and oats that can survive in far northern climates. (14) Many of the crops produced are fodder for livestock. (15) Few nations produce more dairy products than Finland. (16) Almost ten percent of the total exports consists of agricultural products, mostly dairy products. (17) Finnish cheese is exported to many countries. (18) The most important agricultural product is timber. (19) Many farms contain twice as much timberland as farmland. (20) Farmers harvest timber during the winter.

(21) As might be expected, Finland is one of the world's leading producers and exporters of wood products. (22) From Finland's vast forests come not only raw lumber but also finished wood products such as furniture. (23) Wood pulp for making paper is another major forest product. (24) Finland is among the top ten paper producers in the world.

(25) Finland manufactures many types of machinery, including some of the biggest diesel-engine icebreakers in the world, as well as trains, locomotives, and tractors. (26) Icebreakers are shipped to Sweden, Germany, and the Soviet Union. (27) Many sporting rifles in the United States come from Finland.

(28) The hardy Finns have turned their winters to advantage. (29) During the grim winter nights, the Finns do more than their share of merrymaking. (30) Before celebrating Christmas, most people attend anywhere from ten to twenty "Little Christmases." (31) These are parties, complete with the Finnish version of Santa Claus, held at offices and homes. (32) Professional "Santa Clauses" are so much in demand that they advertise their services in the newspapers.

(33) Long winter nights have also helped make the Finns the greatest readers in the world. (34) The people of Helsinki, the capital, claim to have the largest bookstore in the world. (35) The Finns are supposed to be the only people who are one hundred percent literate. (36) They have also taken advantage of the long winters to become expert skiers. (37) The Finns make good use of their long winters!

1. Is Finland a neighbor of Sweden?

   Sentence   (1)   (2)   (3)   (4)   (5)

2. How many lakes are there in Finland?

   Sentence   (5)   (6)   (7)   (8)   (9)

3. Is one-third of Finland north of the Arctic Circle?

   Sentence   (9)   (10)   (11)   (12)   (13)

4. What are two of the obstacles that Finnish farmers face?

   Sentence   (12)   (13)   (14)   (15)   (16)

5. What is the most important agricultural product?

   Sentence   (17)   (18)   (19)   (20)   (21)

6. Do the Finns use any of their lumber for making furniture?

   Sentence   (20)   (21)   (22)   (23)   (24)

7. Is any farm equipment manufactured in Finland?

   Sentence   (25)   (26)   (27)   (28)   (29)

8. Where do "Santa Clauses" advertise?

   Sentence   (28)   (29)   (30)   (31)   (32)

9. What special distinction does Helsinki have?

   Sentence   (31)   (32)   (33)   (34)   (35)

10. How have the seasons affected sports in Finland?

    Sentence   (33)   (34)   (35)   (36)   (37)

UNIT 5
Rich Coast

(1) Spain explored and conquered many areas of Central and South America in the 1500s. (2) The Spaniards heard stories about great mineral wealth in one specific location. (3) So they named the area *Costa Rica*, which means "rich coast." (4) They were disappointed to find no gold or silver there. (5) However, the name of the country remains.

(6) There is another kind of wealth on the coast of Costa Rica, however. (7) The land has tropical rain forests, clean sandy beaches, and a variety of beautiful and distinctive animals and plants. (8) It has active volcanoes and rich hardwood forests. (9) The people of Costa Rica have used this wealth to create a series of national parks that are famous worldwide. (10) Costa Ricans have recognized that the environment is a form of wealth.

(11) A group of tall mountain ranges running from northwest to southeast cuts Costa Rica into three areas. (12) The central highlands has much fertile volcanic soil and a temperate climate. (13) One major crop grown there is coffee. (14) About three fourths of the country's people live in this area. (15) The Caribbean lowlands consists of tropical jungles, or rain forests. (16) Sea turtles come here to lay and hatch their eggs. (17) Tourists also flock to this coast to swim and dive in the clear waters. (18) The Pacific coastal strip is a lowland area on the west coast. (19) The climate there is good for growing bananas.

(20) The people of Costa Rica have varied backgrounds. (21) Ninety-seven percent of the population consists of mestizos and whites. (22) Mestizos are descendants of Spanish colonists and native people who first lived in Costa Rica. (23) There are also two small minority groups. (24) Jamaican blacks live along the Caribbean coast. (25) They are the descendants of Jamaicans who came to build railroads and work on banana plantations about a century ago. (26) Native people make up the second group. (27) They live a traditional life in the highland areas along both coasts. (28) Most Costa Ricans speak Spanish. (29) Those of Jamaican background also speak a Jamaican form of English.

(30) As in all of Central America, Costa Rica's Indian inhabitants were colonized by the Spanish. (31) In 1821, the colony began to break away from Spain. (32) In 1948, Colonel José Figueres became president. (33) He put a Civil Guard in place of the army. (34) He raised wages and expanded the school system. (35) Today Costa Rica is the only country in Central America without a standing army. (36) Its people are 93 percent literate.

(37) Costa Rica has had democratic governments since 1974. (38) It remains neutral, though friendly, to the United States. (39) Oscar Arias Sanchez served as president from 1986–1990. (40) He developed a peace plan to end the civil wars in Nicaragua, El Salvador, and Guatemala. (41) Though the plan did not end these conflicts, Arias Sanchez won the Nobel Peace Prize in 1987.

UNIT 5
Rich Coast

1. Which European country explored Central America in the 1500s?

    Sentence   **(1)**   **(2)**   **(3)**   **(4)**   **(5)**

2. Are the volcanoes in Costa Rica all inactive?

    Sentence   **(6)**   **(7)**   **(8)**   **(9)**   **(10)**

3. What is the climate like in Costa Rica's central highlands?

    Sentence   **(10)**   **(11)**   **(12)**   **(13)**   **(14)**

4. Is a jungle the same thing as a rain forest?

    Sentence   **(13)**   **(14)**   **(15)**   **(16)**   **(17)**

5. Is the west coast of Costa Rica on the Pacific or the Caribbean?

    Sentence   **(18)**   **(19)**   **(20)**   **(21)**   **(22)**

6. Who are the mestizos in Costa Rica?

    Sentence   **(22)**   **(23)**   **(24)**   **(25)**   **(26)**

7. Does any group of Costa Ricans speak English?

    Sentence   **(27)**   **(28)**   **(29)**   **(30)**   **(31)**

8. Did Costa Rican workers make more or less money under Figueres?

    Sentence   **(31)**   **(32)**   **(33)**   **(34)**   **(35)**

9. Is there much illiteracy in Costa Rica?

    Sentence   **(36)**   **(37)**   **(38)**   **(39)**   **(40)**

10. Did the peace plan that Sanchez developed resolve the conflict between other Central American countries?

    Sentence   **(37)**   **(38)**   **(39)**   **(40)**   **(41)**

UNIT 6
Saudi Arabia

(1) Few places in the world present to a visitor as many contrasts as Saudi Arabia does. (2) Here people in cars drive past camel riders, and old houses made of mud share streets with modern high-rise apartment buildings. (3) This country is changing quickly, and it is celebrating its success while feeling the growing pains. (4) Two of the more obvious changes are the result of land use and economic boom—oil wells and cities springing out of the desert.

(5) Nearly half of Saudi Arabia is covered by dry deserts. (6) There are two major desert areas: one, the Northern Deserts, consists of An Nafud and the Syrian Desert; the other is the huge, sandy Rub al Khali. (7) Few people live in these areas, and not much can grow in the desert climate. (8) Some desert dwellers raise livestock for dairy products, but very little land can be used for farming.

(9) In the first half of the twentieth century, Saudi Arabia's deserts became very important. (10) The reason was oil. (11) Deep under the dry sand lie the world's largest oil deposits. (12) Around the world more and more cars and other machines required oil. (13) By exporting and selling oil to other countries, Saudi Arabia brought in vast amounts of money very quickly. (14) These funds gave the country a chance to build better schools and homes for its people.

(15) Most of the people in Saudi Arabia now live in cities. (16) Cities began to grow rapidly at first, but now the growth has slowed down. (17) Many people still live in farming villages, mostly in the western highland region. (18) Some Saudi Arabians are nomads. (19) Nomads are people who wander through the desert with herds of camels, goats, and sheep. (20) Often traveling in groups, they search for water and grazing land, camping along the way. (21) There are fewer nomads today than in the past because many have moved to cities and farms.

(22) Since so much of Saudi Arabia is desert, only one percent of the land is used for farming. (23) Although modern technology has helped bring water to the land, Saudi Arabia must import most of its food. (24) The crops grown include dates, rice, wheat, and vegetables; and an important seafood product is shrimp from the Persian Gulf.

(25) Life has become very different in Saudi Arabia since the oil boom. (26) The country is now involved in other industries besides oil. (27) One major source of income is the money spent by visitors. (28) A large portion of these visitors are not tourists in the usual sense of the word. (29) They come to Saudi Arabia for religious reasons. (30) Two cities, Mecca and Medina, are considered to be the holiest of cities. (31) Over the years many millions of the faithful have visited these religious sites on trips called pilgrimages.

(32) Changes continue to happen in Saudi Arabia, sometimes with a jarring effect. (33) As some Saudis have adopted more Western styles of dress, other people have become upset. (34) The role of women is also changing and has become an important issue. (35) Traditionally, the position of women has been important in the home but not in public. (36) Women were not allowed to have jobs. (37) These days, however, many Saudi Arabian women have become more like those in other industrialized countries. (38) They have joined the work force and are now demanding more rights. (39) Keeping the delicate balance of old and new ways is one of the most difficult tasks for today's Saudi Arabians.

UNIT 6
Saudi Arabia

1. Will visitors find Saudi Arabia a land of many contrasts?

   Sentence   **(1)**   **(2)**   **(3)**   **(4)**   **(5)**

2. How much of Saudi Arabia is covered by deserts?

   Sentence   **(5)**   **(6)**   **(7)**   **(8)**   **(9)**

3. Did the world require oil for cars and other machines?

   Sentence   **(9)**   **(10)**   **(11)**   **(12)**   **(13)**

4. Where do most people in Saudi Arabia live?

   Sentence   **(12)**   **(13)**   **(14)**   **(15)**   **(16)**

5. Who are the nomads?

   Sentence   **(16)**   **(17)**   **(18)**   **(19)**   **(20)**

6. Why are there fewer nomads today?

   Sentence   **(18)**   **(19)**   **(20)**   **(21)**   **(22)**

7. Does Saudi Arabia import much food?

   Sentence   **(19)**   **(20)**   **(21)**   **(22)**   **(23)**

8. Are all visitors to Saudi Arabia considered tourists?

   Sentence   **(26)**   **(27)**   **(28)**   **(29)**   **(30)**

9. What has been the most important traditional role for women?

   Sentence   **(31)**   **(32)**   **(33)**   **(34)**   **(35)**

10. What is a difficult task for today's Saudi Arabians?

    Sentence   **(35)**   **(36)**   **(37)**   **(38)**   **(39)**

In Units 1 through 6, you read about the countries of Turkey, Switzerland, the Soviet Union, Finland, Israel, and Saudi Arabia. You can find books about these countries in the card catalog of a library. A card catalog helps you find any book in the library.

A. Exercising Your Skill

Think about the kinds of information you can find on the cards in a card catalog. Choose six phrases from the box to complete a word map on your paper like the one below. Write the phrases at the ends of the lines. Take guesses if you are not sure.

authors' names	book reports	book titles
publishers' names	calendars	publication dates
Dewey decimal numbers	subjects of books	photographs

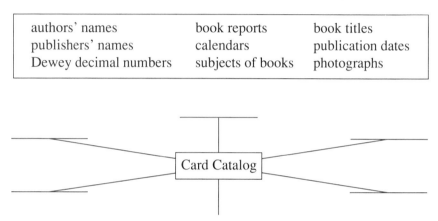

Card Catalog

B. Expanding Your Skill

Every fiction book has an author card and a title card in the card catalog. Every nonfiction book has an author card, a title card, and a subject card. You can use a title card when you know the title of a book. You can use an author card to find all the books by one author or when you know the author but not the title of a book. You can use a subject card to find books about a particular subject.

Read items 1 through 8. On your paper, number from 1 through 8. Tell how you would locate the information listed for each number. Next to each number, write *A* if you would use an author card, *T* if you would use a title card, or *S* if you would use a subject card.

1. a book about space exploration
2. books by Peggy Parish
3. a book called *Aesop's Fables*
4. a science fiction book by Madeleine L'Engle
5. a book called *Moby Dick*
6. a book about whales
7. the latest book by Scott O'Dell
8. a book about robots

C. Exploring Language

Look at these examples of card catalog cards. On your paper, write four questions for each card that can be answered with information from that card.

590	Troubles of Turtles
	Schiff, E.R.
	Costa Publishing
	1989

590.1	Elad, Dana
	Talk About Turtles
	Dooling Publishing Co.
	1990

590.2	TURTLES
	Frost, Allen
	World of Turtles
	Dews Pub. Co., Inc.
	1990

D. Expressing Yourself

Choose one of these activities.

1. Make up author cards for yourself on three books that you might like to write. Use the sketch below as a guide. Use your imagination for book titles and publishing information.

    ```
    (name)
    (title)
    (publishing company)
    (publishing date)
    ```

2. Make a reading guide for a friend or classmate. First list the titles of your five favorite books. For each book write a one- or two-sentence summary of what the book is about. Then, using the library card catalog, write the information needed to find the book in the library.

UNIT 7
Land of 250 Languages

(1) It is the most populous country in Africa and the eighth most populous in the world. (2) Yet it has existed as an independent nation only since 1960. (3) It is Nigeria, a land twice the size of California, located on the west coast of tropical Africa.

(4) No one knows just how many people Nigeria has. (5) Some estimates say 77 million, others as many as 110 million. (6) It is known that Nigeria contains one-fourth of all the people of Africa below the Sahara Desert. (7) They belong mostly to three nation-tribes. (8) In the north there are the Hausa-Fulani people, who practice the Muslim religion. (9) In the west are the Yorubas, and in the east the Ibos. (10) In addition to three separate languages spoken by these groups, there are throughout the nation 250 other languages used by ethnic minorities! (11) To avoid confusion, the government has chosen English and Hausa as the country's official languages. (12) Nigeria was a British colony before it gained independence. (13) Most Nigerians can speak more than one of the country's tongues.

(14) Despite its tropical latitude, Nigeria is far from being all jungle. (15) In the northwest are low, fertile, rainy plains, where a variety of crops are grown. (16) Much of the interior of the country consists of grassy highlands, plateaus, and rugged mountains. (17) Only in the south, toward the coast, is the land thickly forested or swampy. (18) Even though the south is closer to the equator, the north is hotter and drier. (19) Through the heart of Nigeria and into the Atlantic Ocean flows the mighty Niger River.

(20) Three out of four Nigerians live in the countryside. (21) Most of them are farmers, fishers, or herders. (22) They live in small homes made of grass, wood, or dried mud. (23) Mostly, they wear traditional clothing. (24) For both men and women this may consist of long, loose-fitting robes. (25) The men often wear small round caps, and the women wrap cloths called turbans around their heads.

(26) In the cities, however, the way of life is more like our own. (27) Most of the people wear American- or European-style clothes. (28) Lagos, the capital, is a bustling modern city of over a million inhabitants and mammoth traffic jams. (29) In the last twenty years thousands of Nigerians have moved from the hills and plains to the cities. (30) In both city and country, soccer is the Nigerians' favorite sport.

(31) Nigeria is fortunate to have large deposits of petroleum. (32) As income from oil exports rose in the 1970s, a new prosperity came to the nation.

(33) Besides petroleum, Nigeria exports cacao, palm oil, peanuts, rubber, and tin. (34) But petroleum accounts for ninety-five percent of the value of the nation's exports. (35) This new oil wealth has certainly changed the economy. (36) In this varied country, however, many lives go on unchanged.

UNIT 7
Land of 250 Languages

1. How does this country rank in population in Africa?

   Sentence   **(1)**   **(2)**   **(3)**   **(4)**   **(5)**

2. Do estimates of Nigeria's population rise over a million?

   Sentence   **(5)**   **(6)**   **(7)**   **(8)**   **(9)**

3. What are the official languages of Nigeria?

   Sentence   **(8)**   **(9)**   **(10)**   **(11)**   **(12)**

4. Can many Nigerians speak more than one language?

   Sentence   **(10)**   **(11)**   **(12)**   **(13)**   **(14)**

5. Where in Nigeria are a variety of crops grown?

   Sentence   **(15)**   **(16)**   **(17)**   **(18)**   **(19)**

6. Do most people live in the country?

   Sentence   **(18)**   **(19)**   **(20)**   **(21)**   **(22)**

7. What are the chief occupations of Nigerians?

   Sentence   **(21)**   **(22)**   **(23)**   **(24)**   **(25)**

8. Does city life in Nigeria resemble our city life?

   Sentence   **(26)**   **(27)**   **(28)**   **(29)**   **(30)**

9. Are there deposits of petroleum in the ground?

   Sentence   **(28)**   **(29)**   **(30)**   **(31)**   **(32)**

10. Do the Nigerians export any rubber?

    Sentence   **(32)**   **(33)**   **(34)**   **(35)**   **(36)**

(1) Ireland, an island in the North Atlantic Ocean just west of Great Britain, is known as the "Emerald Isle." (2) The name is given to Ireland because of its beautiful green pastures. (3) St. George's Channel, the North Channel, the Atlantic Ocean, and the Irish Sea wash the shores of Ireland. (4) Since 1922 Ireland has been divided into the six counties of Northern Ireland (part of the United Kingdom) and the twenty-six counties of the Irish Free State, now officially the Republic of Ireland.

(5) Northern Ireland occupies about seventeen percent of the island of Ireland. (6) It contains about thirty percent of the island's people. (7) Northern Ireland is more industrialized than the Republic. (8) A large concentration of its people live in cities (about thirty percent in Belfast), and manufactured goods are the mainstay of its economy. (9) Shipbuilding and the manufacture of aircraft and fine linen are leading sources of income. (10) Its chief exports include clothing, textiles, food, and machinery.

(11) In the Republic of Ireland the economy is based largely on agriculture. (12) Most farms are small. (13) Almost two-thirds of its farmlands are devoted to grazing. (14) Livestock constitutes its chief product. (15) About three-quarters of its cattle are exported, but most of the foodstuffs are eaten at home.

(16) Peat bogs cover about one-seventh of the Irish Republic. (17) Peat bogs are swampy lands made up of decaying plants. (18) They occur where drainage is poor. (19) Peat is widely used as a fuel in Ireland. (20) Before it can be of use, it must be cut from the ground in slablike blocks, drained, and dried. (21) It is often moist when first gathered. (22) Peat is used in lands where coal and wood are insufficient for local fuel needs.

(23) For a long time Ireland was one of the few countries whose population was decreasing. (24) The country today still has fewer people than it did in the early 1800s. (25) A great famine in the late 1840s caused a wave of Irish emigrants to depart for the United States, Canada, and other lands in the Western Hemisphere. (26) A population of over six million shrank to less than three million, but in recent years it has started to grow again. (27) Even so, there are more people of Irish descent in the United States today than there are in Ireland.

(28) The list of famous Irish would be lengthy indeed. (29) Foremost are those who have excelled in literature. (30) William Butler Yeats, George Russell, George Bernard Shaw, and Lady Augusta Gregory were outstanding literary figures at the turn of the century. (31) Modern Irish writers who have achieved fame include James Joyce, Sean O'Casey, and Frank O'Connor. (32) The long tradition of famous authors continues with recent figures such as Brendan Behan.

(33) Tourism is rapidly becoming an important part of Ireland's economy. (34) Millions of tourists visit Ireland each year. (35) Many come from the United States. (36) Some come to see their ancestral homes, and others arrive to see rural, quaint, beautiful Ireland itself. (37) Its hospitable citizens say, "A hundred thousand welcomes." (38) Few visitors resist its bewitching charm.

1. Why is Ireland called the "Emerald Isle"?

   Sentence   **(1)**   **(2)**   **(3)**   **(4)**   **(5)**

2. What percentage of Ireland's population lives in Northern Ireland?

   Sentence   **(5)**   **(6)**   **(7)**   **(8)**   **(9)**

3. Are the farms large in the Republic of Ireland?

   Sentence   **(9)**   **(10)**   **(11)**   **(12)**   **(13)**

4. Are any foods exported?

   Sentence   **(13)**   **(14)**   **(15)**   **(16)**   **(17)**

5. What are peat bogs composed of?

   Sentence   **(17)**   **(18)**   **(19)**   **(20)**   **(21)**

6. In what kinds of countries is peat used as a fuel?

   Sentence   **(20)**   **(21)**   **(22)**   **(23)**   **(24)**

7. Is the population of Ireland still decreasing?

   Sentence   **(23)**   **(24)**   **(25)**   **(26)**   **(27)**

8. In what field have the Irish excelled?

   Sentence   **(26)**   **(27)**   **(28)**   **(29)**   **(30)**

9. Who are three famous modern Irish writers?

   Sentence   **(29)**   **(30)**   **(31)**   **(32)**   **(33)**

10. Why do Irish-Americans visit Ireland?

    Sentence   **(34)**   **(35)**   **(36)**   **(37)**   **(38)**

UNIT 9
Land of Prosperity

(**1**) Sweden, about the size of California, occupies the eastern half of the Scandinavian peninsula. (**2**) It shares boundaries with Norway and Finland. (**3**) Just under a thousand miles long and about 250 miles wide, Sweden is by far the largest Scandinavian country. (**4**) About one-seventh of the country lies above the Arctic Circle.

(**5**) Sweden is very mountainous. (**6**) Because trees cover more than half of the land and there is a short growing season, little of Sweden is ideally suited for farming. (**7**) The land that is suited for farming, less than ten percent, is intensively cultivated. (**8**) Grains such as wheat, oats, and barley are the principal crops. (**9**) In spite of its limited farmland, Sweden is able to supply all its own food. (**10**) Because of its skilled workers and scientific farming methods, Sweden's crop yield per acre is one of the highest in the world.

(**11**) Forestry plays the most important role in the nation's economy. (**12**) Only Canada competes with Sweden for the world's leadership in lumbering, pulpwood, and allied industries. (**13**) In Sweden more land is covered by forests than in any other European country except the Soviet Union.

(**14**) Much of Sweden's forestland lies in the north. (**15**) Northern Sweden, known as Norrland, is a sparsely settled region of high mountains, beautiful lakes, and vast forests. (**16**) Norrland comprises sixty percent of the entire country. (**17**) In this area nearly everyone works in the woods part of the year, felling trees and transporting them to the great sawmills located along the coast. (**18**) In Sweden timber is made into everything from matches and mousetraps to furniture.

(**19**) Life in Lapland, the northern province of Norrland, is stern and grim. (**20**) Winter is much too cold and summer far too short for much farming. (**21**) In this region the Lapps still roam the tundra with their reindeer herds, much as their ancestors did centuries ago. (**22**) Often called the "Land of the Midnight Sun," Lapland has a bright sky day and night during the months of June and July. (**23**) In winter the opposite occurs; no sun at all is seen over the horizon during December and January.

(**24**) Educational standards are high. (**25**) Ninety-nine out of every hundred Swedish adults can read and write. (**26**) From the fifth grade on, the children must study English. (**27**) All children must attend school for nine years. (**28**) Adult schools are numerous for those who wish to further their education. (**29**) Every large organizational group—labor, farmers, and others—provides its own form of adult education. (**30**) With an excellent educational system, adequate natural resources, and an industrious people, Sweden has reached a high standard of living.

(**31**) Tourists who visit Sweden each year number over half a million. (**32**) They return to their native lands with enthusiastic tales of the natural beauty of the land and of the good living enjoyed by its industrious inhabitants.

UNIT 9
Land of Prosperity

1. Which is the largest Scandinavian country?

   Sentence   **(1)**   **(2)**   **(3)**   **(4)**   **(5)**

2. What are the main crops?

   Sentence   **(6)**   **(7)**   **(8)**   **(9)**   **(10)**

3. Does Sweden have to import food?

   Sentence   **(9)**   **(10)**   **(11)**   **(12)**   **(13)**

4. What is northern Sweden called?

   Sentence   **(12)**   **(13)**   **(14)**   **(15)**   **(16)**

5. Is life pleasant in Lapland?

   Sentence   **(15)**   **(16)**   **(17)**   **(18)**   **(19)**

6. For how many months is Lapland without sun?

   Sentence   **(19)**   **(20)**   **(21)**   **(22)**   **(23)**

7. Is English taught in Swedish schools?

   Sentence   **(23)**   **(24)**   **(25)**   **(26)**   **(27)**

8. Are adult-education programs throughout the country identical?

   Sentence   **(25)**   **(26)**   **(27)**   **(28)**   **(29)**

9. Does Sweden have an excellent educational system?

   Sentence   **(26)**   **(27)**   **(28)**   **(29)**   **(30)**

10. Is a good life obvious to visitors?

    Sentence   **(28)**   **(29)**   **(30)**   **(31)**   **(32)**

UNIT 10
Land of the Past

(1) Peru, South America's third largest country, can be broken into three distinct regions. (2) The coastal plain area, where most of its ports and cities are located, faces the Pacific Ocean. (3) Inland lie the Andes Mountains, among the most rugged in the world. (4) This region covers about two-fifths of the nation's total land area. (5) Farther east lie the low, tropical rain forests. (6) These three regions differ so widely in climate and land surface that each forms, in effect, a world to itself.

(7) The coastal plain is a narrow ribbon of barren, dry land. (8) For the most part, it consists of sand and rocks. (9) In some sections of this region, years go by without a single rainfall. (10) The only plant life is found where streams empty into the ocean. (11) There, with the help of irrigation, valuable crops can be grown—largely rice, sugar cane, and cotton.

(12) East of the coastal plain lie the towering Andes Mountains. (13) The snow-capped Andes form a barrier between the western coast and the eastern rain forests. (14) Varying elevations in the Andes permit a variety of crops to be grown. (15) In the deep valleys tropical plants can be raised. (16) Grains and potatoes are grown in higher areas. (17) In still higher areas, where cultivation becomes difficult, sheep and cattle are grazed. (18) Beyond that lie only jagged, glittering mountain peaks.

(19) To the east of the Andes, the land is carpeted with trees. (20) The vast forests cover half of the total area of the country. (21) Few people live in this hot, humid area. (22) Enormous amounts of timber are made almost valueless because of the difficulty of transporting them to market.

(23) Forming part of the boundary between Peru and Bolivia is the highest major lake in the world. (24) The giant "Lake Above the Clouds" is 110 miles long and 40 miles wide. (25) Here the world's loftiest regular steamship service has been established. (26) Lake Titicaca is extremely deep, in some places over twelve hundred feet. (27) Beneath its waters lie the ruins of an ancient Indian civilization only recently discovered by an American deep-sea diver. (28) Along the lake shores can be seen the ruins of the once great Inca civilization.

(29) Long before the Spanish conquerors reached Peru in the 1500s, the Incas had built a powerful and advanced civilization. (30) They were highly skilled in stonework, road building, weaving, and astronomy. (31) Their numerous buildings still standing are monuments to the Incan skill in construction. (32) Indian stone was no match for Spanish steel, however, and the Incan civilization, stricken by internal strife, fell before the Spanish soldiers.

(33) Today many of Peru's people are of Indian blood. (34) They are working to blend the "Land of the Past" with the "Land of Tomorrow."

1. What ocean does Peru's coastal plain face?

    Sentence **(1)**   **(2)**   **(3)**   **(4)**   **(5)**

2. In which direction are the rain forests?

    Sentence **(4)**   **(5)**   **(6)**   **(7)**   **(8)**

3. What valuable crops are grown on the coastal plain?

    Sentence **(7)**   **(8)**   **(9)**   **(10)**   **(11)**

4. What mountains form a barrier between the coast and the eastern rain forests?

    Sentence **(10)**   **(11)**   **(12)**   **(13)**   **(14)**

5. Is cultivation difficult in the higher areas?

    Sentence **(13)**   **(14)**   **(15)**   **(16)**   **(17)**

6. Have the Andes Mountains been worn smooth by the effects of weather?

    Sentence **(16)**   **(17)**   **(18)**   **(19)**   **(20)**

7. Do many people live in the hot, humid eastern area?

    Sentence **(20)**   **(21)**   **(22)**   **(23)**   **(24)**

8. What is unique about transportation on Lake Titicaca?

    Sentence **(24)**   **(25)**   **(26)**   **(27)**   **(28)**

9. Was the Incan civilization highly developed prior to the Spanish conquest?

    Sentence **(27)**   **(28)**   **(29)**   **(30)**   **(31)**

10. Was Indian stone any match for Spanish steel?

    Sentence **(30)**   **(31)**   **(32)**   **(33)**   **(34)**

UNIT 11
The Kiwi People

(1) In the western Pacific, halfway between the equator and the South Pole, lies New Zealand. (2) It consists of two main islands and many smaller ones in the neighboring seas. (3) The two main islands, North Island and South Island, are separated by the sixteen-mile-wide Cook Strait. (4) The long and narrow land stretches a thousand miles from north to south. (5) Far to the east across six thousand miles of water lies South America. (6) Twelve hundred miles to the west lies Australia.

(7) Like other lands that have long been cut off from the rest of the world, New Zealand has developed unique plant and animal life. (8) Most interesting are some of the animals. (9) New Zealand alone is the home of the strange, flightless kiwi. (10) This chicken-sized bird has been declared the national symbol and appears on one of the country's coins. (11) New Zealand is also the home of a sheep-killing parrot. (12) One species of lizardlike creatures, the tuatara, is the sole survivor of an ancient order of reptiles. (13) A striking peculiarity of the tuatara is the presence of a third eye on the top of its head!

(14) Two-thirds of New Zealand is devoted to agriculture and the raising of livestock. (15) The country, one of the world's leading rural areas, contains over twelve million acres of grazing land. (16) On these lands graze eight million cattle and sixty-five million sheep. (17) No other country has as many farm animals in proportion to its population. (18) Almost all of the 600 million pounds of wool produced each year is exported.

(19) New Zealand's foreign trade is one of the world's highest in proportion to its population. (20) Almost forty percent of all that New Zealand produces is shipped to foreign markets. (21) Wool, mutton, lamb, skins and hides, and dairy products account for ninety percent of its exports. (22) New Zealand is the world's biggest exporter of dairy products. (23) It is the second largest in exporting meat and the third largest in exporting wool. (24) Almost seventy-five percent of the exports go to members of the British Commonwealth of Nations. (25) From this small country, about the size of Colorado, Great Britain receives thirty percent of its meat imports, forty percent of its imported butter, and fifty percent of its cheese imports.

(26) New Zealand was first seen by a European in the year 1642. (27) A Dutch navigator, Abel Tasman, sighted South Island but did not go ashore because of the hostility of the natives, a race of Polynesians called Maori. (28) According to tradition, the Maoris migrated from other Pacific islands to New Zealand in the 1300s. (29) When other people were unwilling to journey out of sight of land, daring Maoris were traveling over wide expanses of the Pacific in fragile outrigger canoes. (30) The Maoris made New Zealand their home. (31) They have lived there ever since.

(32) For many years after the arrival of the Europeans, the number of Maoris declined. (33) Today their numbers are increasing, and they have taken up the ways of the European settlers. (34) Proud of being New Zealanders, they say, "After all, we were the first of the Kiwi People."

1. Where is New Zealand located?

    Sentence   (1)   (2)   (3)   (4)   (5)

2. What has New Zealand developed?

    Sentence   (4)   (5)   (6)   (7)   (8)

3. Which are more fascinating, the plants or the animals?

    Sentence   (7)   (8)   (9)   (10)   (11)

4. How much grazing land does New Zealand have?

    Sentence   (11)   (12)   (13)   (14)   (15)

5. Does the number of sheep exceed the number of cattle?

    Sentence   (14)   (15)   (16)   (17)   (18)

6. How much wool is exported annually?

    Sentence   (17)   (18)   (19)   (20)   (21)

7. Are exports sent to the British Commonwealth of Nations?

    Sentence   (20)   (21)   (22)   (23)   (24)

8. Why didn't Tasman go ashore?

    Sentence   (23)   (24)   (25)   (26)   (27)

9. When did the Maoris migrate to New Zealand?

    Sentence   (27)   (28)   (29)   (30)   (31)

10. What happened to the Maoris in the years immediately following the coming of the Europeans?

    Sentence   (30)   (31)   (32)   (33)   (34)

UNIT 12
Old Land—New Country

(1) Ukraine is one of the republics formed by the breakup of the Soviet Union. (2) The second largest republic, it is smaller only than Russia. (3) Ukraine is on the Black Sea in southern Europe. (4) Its capital is Kiev.

(5) Of Ukraine's fifty-three million people, three fourths are ethnic Ukrainians. (6) The second largest population in Ukraine is Russians. (7) Other groups include Jews, Bulgarians, and Poles.

(8) Like the United States, Ukraine has large plains. (9) They are called *steppes*. (10) They contain much fertile soil, which makes Ukraine a major farming region. (11) The American and Canadian plains are called the "breadbasket of the world" because of their high production of agricultural products. (12) Similarly, Ukraine is known as the "breadbasket of Europe."

(13) Ukrainian people love sports. (14) These include volleyball, basketball, ice hockey, track and field, and soccer. (15) Soccer is the most popular sport. (16) The Ukrainian team, Kiev Dynamo, is one of Europe's leading soccer teams. (17) On a more sedate level, many Ukrainians play chess.

(18) Ukraine has a history of colorful folk art. (19) Their brightly colored Easter eggs are known throughout the world. (20) Music and dance are also popular. (21) Singing in choral groups is a popular activity for many Ukrainians. (22) Ukrainian poets and writers have given the Ukrainian language literary importance.

(23) The country has also tried to use Ukrainian language more in schools. (24) The percentage of Ukrainian students learning in the Ukrainian language has been increasing since 1989. (25) Students attend school from age 7 to 18. (26) Some go on to higher education at one of the nine universities.

(27) Ukraine has long sought independence from Soviet control. (28) During the 1960s, protest movements led to the arrest of thousands of human rights advocates. (29) The protests continued through the breakup of the Soviet Union. (30) In 1990 the parliament of Ukraine declared sovereignty. (31) This meant that if Ukraine's laws conflicted with those of the Soviet Union, the republic would follow its own laws.

(32) In 1986, the Chernobyl nuclear power plant in Ukraine exploded, releasing large amounts of radioactive material over many miles. (33) Although Soviet officials said only a few people died or were harmed, Ukrainian sources estimate much higher death and injury rates. (34) Many areas near the plant had to be evacuated. (35) Today these areas are still too radioactive for people to live there safely. (36) The effects of radiation have caused cancer in many people in Ukraine and the republics of Russia and Belarus. (37) Environmental activists in Ukraine have joined others around the world to try to shut down such nuclear plants.

UNIT 12
Old Land—New Country

1. Is Ukraine larger or smaller than Russia?

   Sentence   **(1)**   **(2)**   **(3)**   **(4)**   **(5)**

2. What are the Ukrainian plains called?

   Sentence   **(5)**   **(6)**   **(7)**   **(8)**   **(9)**

3. What is Ukraine's agricultural nickname?

   Sentence   **(9)**   **(10)**   **(11)**   **(12)**   **(13)**

4. Is hockey the most popular sport in Ukraine?

   Sentence   **(13)**   **(14)**   **(15)**   **(16)**   **(17)**

5. Which Ukraine folk art has international fame?

   Sentence   **(17)**   **(18)**   **(19)**   **(20)**   **(21)**

6. Are any books printed in the Ukrainian language?

   Sentence   **(20)**   **(21)**   **(22)**   **(23)**   **(24)**

7. Is Ukraine's struggle for independence a recent happening?

   Sentence   **(24)**   **(25)**   **(26)**   **(27)**   **(28)**

8. When did Ukraine declare sovereignty?

   Sentence   **(27)**   **(28)**   **(29)**   **(30)**   **(31)**

9. With whom was Ukraine's sovereignty battle fought?

   Sentence   **(30)**   **(31)**   **(32)**   **(33)**   **(34)**

10. Can people live safely near the area of Chernobyl today?

    Sentence   **(32)**   **(33)**   **(34)**   **(35)**   **(36)**

A. Exercising Your Skill

In Units 7 through 12, you read about the countries of Nigeria, Ireland, Sweden, Peru, New Zealand, and Liberia. You read these passages for pleasure and to gather information. You could also have scanned or skimmed the material.

When you **scan** a passage, you move your eyes quickly over the material until you find the fact or facts you are looking for. When you **skim** a passage, you read the material quickly to get the main idea.

On your paper, write each of the phrases below under the heading Scan or Skim to tell how you would get the information from a piece of written material.

- the date of a battle
- why a leader was popular
- the number of voters in a particular election
- why a colony survived
- the major crop of an area
- why one event led to another event

B. Expanding Your Skill

Read the following questions. Number your paper from 1 to 15. Write *scan* or *skim* to tell how you would read to get the required information. If you write *scan*, also write the key word from the question that tells the kind of fact you are looking for.

1. In what year did Nigeria become an independent country?
2. In Nigeria, why is city life different from life in the country?
3. What one product makes up most of Nigeria's exports?
4. What are three of Ireland's chief exports?
5. Why are more people of Irish descent living in the United States than in Ireland?
6. What are the names of two famous Irish authors?
7. When was Ireland divided into two sections?
8. Why is mountainous Sweden able to maintain one of the highest crop yields per acre in the world?
9. How many years of education are required by law in Sweden?
10. What was the pre-sixteenth-century Incan civilization in Peru like?
11. How much of Peru's total land area is in the Andes Mountains?
12. How much wool is produced yearly in New Zealand?
13. Why did the Maori people come to inhabit New Zealand?
14. What group from America first settled the land that is now Liberia?
15. Why do so many ships fly the Liberian flag?

C. Exploring Language

Read the paragraphs below. On your paper, write two or three questions for each paragraph that can be answered by scanning the material in the paragraph.

The ancient Incan city of Machu Picchu was located only 50 miles northwest of the present-day Peruvian city of Cuzco. It was, however, almost 7,000 feet above sea level in the Andes Mountains.

Dominated by the peak of the mountain Huayna Picchu, and with other mountain peaks all around, the city of Machu Picchu itself had at its center a flat plaza. The plaza area was surrounded by stone temples, official buildings, and homes.

In order to survive in the mountain stronghold, the Incas cut flat terraces into the slopes. They built low walls to support them, then planted seeds in the soil on the flat terrace surfaces. These six-foot-wide terrace gardens were called *andennes*, and they received water from an irrigation system developed by the Incas. The *andennes* ran in ribbonlike patterns along the slopes and produced well enough to insure the Incan population of sufficient crops such as corn, potatoes, squash, and beans.

It is not certain, but some believe that the Inca built Machu Picchu as a hideaway from Spanish conquerors then in Cuzco. Machu Picchu was well hidden—so well that it was not discovered by modern explorers until 1911.

D. Expressing Yourself

Choose one of these activities.

1. Choose a newspaper story. Skim the first paragraph to get the main idea of the whole article. Then skim the other paragraphs for their main ideas. Summarize the story with the information you got from skimming. Then read the story more slowly to see if you did, in fact, pick up all the important information by skimming.

2. Choose a chapter in a school book. Write questions that can be answered by scanning section titles within the chapter. Skim one section in the chapter, then write the main idea of that section. Exchange questions and main ideas with a partner. By reading your partner's questions and main idea you should be able to find the chapter.

UNIT 13
A Crowded but Beautiful Land

(1) Imagine half the people of the United States all living in Montana, and you will grasp how small and crowded Japan is. (2) Japan is an island country off the east coast of Asia. (3) It consists of four main islands and 3,300 others, most too tiny or rocky to be inhabited. (4) The main islands form a north-south string about 1,300 miles long—the same distance as from Maine to Florida. (5) Six-sevenths of the land consists of mountains, including forty active volcanoes.

(6) Since so much of Japan is mountainous, the homes of most of its 123 million people are squeezed into the level land along the coasts. (7) The nation's capital, Tokyo, on the east coast, is the world's second most populous metropolitan area. (8) Over eleven million people live there. (9) Japan's steep mountains also leave only about fifteen percent of its land flat enough for agriculture. (10) However, by using modern scientific methods, Japanese farmers produce more crops per acre than any others in the world. (11) Even so, Japan must import over one-third of its food. (12) The sea is another major food source. (13) Fish and rice are staples of the Japanese diet.

(14) The Japanese islands also lack vital mineral resources, such as oil and iron. (15) In order to manufacture goods, Japan must import these and other raw materials. (16) Japan pays for all its imports by producing vast quantities of goods in its factories and exporting them throughout the world. (17) Television sets and other electronic equipment, cameras, automobiles, ships, and clothing are produced with great efficiency.

(18) Japan has not always engaged in commerce with the rest of the world. (19) Legend says that Japan became an empire over 2,600 years ago, under the emperor Jimmu Tenno, a descendant of the sun goddess and ancestor of the present emperor. (20) Yet for about 2,500 of those 2,600 years Japan remained largely isolated from the outside world. (21) Not until an American, Commodore Perry, visited Japan in 1854 did the Japanese begin to trade with the Western world and seek to adopt Western ways. (22) After being devastated in World War II, Japan has made a remarkable comeback and is now the world's third greatest industrial nation.

(23) Japan's mountains, though hindering agriculture, provide the country with scenes of awe-inspiring beauty. (24) The Japanese people have a great love of nature. (25) They delight in taking trips from their modern, crowded cities into the quiet countryside to enjoy the jagged peaks, peaceful valleys, and breeze-swept shores. (26) Most beloved of all their mountains is towering Fuji, an inactive volcano that sweeps upward in a graceful curve to a snowcapped summit. (27) Climbing Fuji is a "must" for millions of Japanese.

(28) Visitors find Japanese life today a fascinating blend of ancient and modern. (29) Most Japanese wear Western-style clothing to work and commute by car, bicycle, bus, or subway. (30) When they arrive home, however, they may change into traditional Japanese robes and slippers and kneel on the floor for their centuries-old tea ceremony. (31) After that ancient ritual they may well sit back, click on their television, and watch Japanese baseball or an American western movie—with the cowhands saying, "Sayonara (so long), partner."

1. How much of the total area of Japan is mountainous?

    Sentence   (1)   (2)   (3)   (4)   (5)

2. What is the population of Japan?

    Sentence   (6)   (7)   (8)   (9)   (10)

3. Is there any land suitable for agriculture?

    Sentence   (8)   (9)   (10)   (11)   (12)

4. Is Japan rich in mineral resources?

    Sentence   (13)   (14)   (15)   (16)   (17)

5. How do the Japanese obtain raw materials for manufacturing?

    Sentence   (15)   (16)   (17)   (18)   (19)

6. Has Japan always engaged in commerce with other countries?

    Sentence   (18)   (19)   (20)   (21)   (22)

7. Are the Japanese people known as nature lovers?

    Sentence   (23)   (24)   (25)   (26)   (27)

8. Is the volcano in Mount Fuji active?

    Sentence   (26)   (27)   (28)   (29)   (30)

9. Do the Japanese live in a totally modern world?

    Sentence   (27)   (28)   (29)   (30)   (31)

10. What does *sayonara* mean?

    Sentence   (27)   (28)   (29)   (30)   (31)

UNIT 14
The Shoelace Country

(1) Long, narrow Chile stretches 2,650 miles along the western coast of South America. (2) Located between the Andes Mountains and the Pacific Ocean, it reaches from Peru on the north to the extreme southern tip of the continent. (3) Yet the "Shoelace Country" averages only 110 miles in width. (4) Ribbonlike Chile is divided into three distinct regions: the northern desert; the rich central region; and the forested, rain-swept south.

(5) Northern Chile begins in the hot Atacama Desert. (6) In this brown, sun-drenched area years may go by without a single shower. (7) Yet this desert holds Chile's principal source of wealth. (8) The world's largest copper and nitrate deposits are there. (9) Miners who work in the dry north do not wish for rain. (10) A downpour could wash away the nitrate. (11) This dry area covers about a third of Chile.

(12) The heart of the nation is central Chile. (13) The majority of Chile's large cities and its people are in or near the Central Valley. (14) Most of the agriculture and manufacturing is carried on here. (15) Cattle raising and some mining are other industries of importance in this area. (16) It has a highly favorable climate.

(17) Cold winds, driving rains, and heavy forests make southern Chile an unattractive place to live. (18) Its population is sparse, less than one person per square mile. (19) Shepherds have wide stretches over which they graze their sheep. (20) The animals' fleece grows thick in the cold, wet air. (21) A dwindling number of primitive Indians still make this wild-appearing, storm-swept area their home.

(22) Chile owns several islands. (23) One, in the Juan Fernandez group, is commonly identified as the island of Robinson Crusoe. (24) Another is lonely Easter Island. (25) On this island, some two thousand miles from Chile, are large stone images built by a vanished people. (26) Why these large statues were constructed still remains a mystery in history. (27) Tierra del Fuego is Chile's large southern island. (28) Located south of the Strait of Magellan, it is for most people an unknown land, parts of which even today remain unexplored. (29) Its southern area toward Cape Horn is bleak and foggy. (30) On this island lies the world's southernmost town, Punta Arenas.

(31) High in the Andes Mountains stands a monument that is known by people the world over, the Christ of the Andes. (32) The tall bronze statue marks the boundary line between Chile and Argentina. (33) For years the two countries quarreled over the boundary. (34) They were about to fight but finally settled the matter in peace. (35) The two nations melted their cannons and erected a statue with the metal. (36) A plate on the base of the statue says in Spanish, "Sooner shall these mountains crumble to dust than the peoples of Argentina and Chile break the peace they have sworn to defend at the feet of Christ, the Redeemer." (37) This solemn vow made in 1904 has not been broken to this day.

UNIT 14
The Shoelace Country

1. What is the average width of Chile?

   Sentence   **(1)**   **(2)**   **(3)**   **(4)**   **(5)**

2. Is copper found in the Atacama Desert?

   Sentence   **(6)**   **(7)**   **(8)**   **(9)**   **(10)**

3. Why don't miners desire rain?

   Sentence   **(9)**   **(10)**   **(11)**   **(12)**   **(13)**

4. Where are the major cities located?

   Sentence   **(12)**   **(13)**   **(14)**   **(15)**   **(16)**

5. Why do so few people live in southern Chile?

   Sentence   **(14)**   **(15)**   **(16)**   **(17)**   **(18)**

6. Is there much land in southern Chile for grazing sheep?

   Sentence   **(19)**   **(20)**   **(21)**   **(22)**   **(23)**

7. What body of water separates Chile from Tierra del Fuego?

   Sentence   **(24)**   **(25)**   **(26)**   **(27)**   **(28)**

8. What is the area toward Cape Horn like?

   Sentence   **(25)**   **(26)**   **(27)**   **(28)**   **(29)**

9. Did Chile and Argentina ever have a dispute over territory?

   Sentence   **(29)**   **(30)**   **(31)**   **(32)**   **(33)**

10. What was made with the metal from the cannons?

    Sentence   **(33)**   **(34)**   **(35)**   **(36)**   **(37)**

UNIT 15
Land of Change

(1) Korea has had a stormy history for such a small land. (2) This country has always been strongly influenced by other countries. (3) It is connected to China, and it is separated from Japan by only a small body of water. (4) Both China and Japan have ruled Korea in the past. (5) In modern times vast changes have occurred in Korea.

(6) Since 1948 there have been two separate nations—North Korea and South Korea. (7) The armies of North Korea invaded South Korea in 1950. (8) Other countries became involved in what grew to be the Korean War. (9) The war ended in 1953, but neither side won, and no peace treaty has ever been signed. (10) At times, however, efforts have been made to unite Korea once again.

(11) The two nations lie on the Korean Peninsula, which is about the same size as the state of Utah. (12) North Korea occupies the northern half and South Korea the southern. (13) Although North Korea is slightly larger than South Korea, South Korea has more than twice as many people.

(14) Plains cover the western, southern, and northeastern coasts. (15) The rest of the peninsula contains mostly mountains. (16) Most Koreans live near the coasts. (17) The coastal plains are good for agriculture. (18) In fact, before the division of the country, farming was the most important means of making money for Korea. (19) Since the country has become divided, both nations have concentrated on industry. (20) Now industry is as important as agriculture. (21) This change has led both countries to have two of the fastest-growing economies in the world.

(22) In general, Korean summers are warm and winters cold. (23) Seasonal winds called monsoons create extremes in the weather. (24) During the summer a hot, wet monsoon blows in from the south, depositing nearly half of Korea's yearly rainfall. (25) The winter monsoon blows an icy wind on both countries, but the lowland plains are protected by the huge Central Mountains.

(26) In both countries life in modern times is very different from life in years past. (27) In North Korea, for example, women have now been encouraged to work outside the home. (28) This was not true in the past. (29) The North Korean government has built day-care centers for children whose mothers work. (30) In South Korea industry has grown rapidly. (31) Nowadays this country can compete in the modern world. (32) During this current period of change, Korea's tradition of "extended families" has continued. (33) Children, parents, and grandparents often live together. (34) This arrangement works well when the parents work. (35) The grandparents take care of the children.

(36) The people of North Korea and South Korea have grown used to change as a way of life. (37) For now, the people of each country are working to help their nation gain a leadership role in the world's economy. (38) In their different ways, both countries are succeeding.

UNIT 15
Land of Change

1. Has Korea been influenced by other countries?

   Sentence   (1)   (2)   (3)   (4)   (5)

2. Is Korea now two separate nations?

   Sentence   (3)   (4)   (5)   (6)   (7)

3. Have efforts been made to unite Korea again?

   Sentence   (7)   (8)   (9)   (10)   (11)

4. Which country is larger, North Korea or South Korea?

   Sentence   (10)   (11)   (12)   (13)   (14)

5. Since division, what have both countries concentrated on?

   Sentence   (15)   (16)   (17)   (18)   (19)

6. What are monsoons?

   Sentence   (20)   (21)   (22)   (23)   (24)

7. How does life in both countries today compare to life in the past?

   Sentence   (25)   (26)   (27)   (28)   (29)

8. Does the "extended family" help working parents?

   Sentence   (30)   (31)   (32)   (33)   (34)

9. How have North and South Koreans reacted to change?

   Sentence   (33)   (34)   (35)   (36)   (37)

10. Are both countries succeeding in gaining economic leadership?

    Sentence   (34)   (35)   (36)   (37)   (38)

UNIT 16
Big "Little Venice"

(1) When European explorers landed on the northern coast of South America in the 1500s, they found Indian houses built on sticks in the water along sea and lake shores. (2) This reminded them of how the Italian city of Venice is built. (3) Thus they called the land Venezuela, which in Spanish means "Little Venice." (4) Today Venezuela is one of the most modern and prosperous nations in South America.

(5) Venezuela is about twice the size of California. (6) Its borders form roughly an upside-down triangle. (7) The base of the triangle faces the Caribbean Sea on the north. (8) Although much of this region is mountainous, most of the country's people live there. (9) Along the west side of the triangle lies Colombia. (10) Along the east lie Guyana and Brazil. (11) The point of the triangle aims south toward the heart of South America. (12) In the center of the triangle is a broad area of plains called the Llanos. (13) These plains are drained by the great Orinoco River, 1,300 miles long. (14) On the Llanos are extensive cattle ranches and farms.

(15) The history of Venezuela has been a long and, until recent years, not a very happy one. (16) The original inhabitants were the Carib and Arawak Indians. (17) Columbus made his first landing on the mainland of the Americas there in 1498. (18) The Spanish settled and ruled the land until the early 1800s. (19) It was one of Spain's poorest colonies. (20) The great liberator, Simón Bolívar, led Venezuela to independence in 1821. (21) But poverty was still widespread until the 1920s. (22) At that time Venezuela realized that it had vast resources of what the industrialized world needed more and more—oil.

(23) Its petroleum deposits have transformed Venezuela from one of South America's poorest countries into one of its richest. (24) Today it is the world's fifth largest exporter of oil. (25) Only Saudi Arabia, Iraq, Iran, and the Soviet Union export more. (26) Over ninety percent of Venezuela's export earnings come from oil. (27) Much of the oil is under huge Lake Maracaibo in the northwest. (28) Hundreds of oil wells have been erected in the lake itself. (29) They look like a forest of burned-out Christmas trees jutting out of the water.

(30) Because of Venezuela's petroleum, a large portion of its seventeen million people enjoy a comfortable standard of living. (31) The capital city, Caracas, presents a skyline of modern office towers and high-rise apartment houses. (32) The people enjoy baseball, soccer, rodeos, and dancing the *joropo*. (33) Yet much poverty remains. (34) Hillsides in and around the large cities are often crowded with slum shacks called *ranchos*. (35) The government is using some of its wealth to improve housing, jobs, and education for the poor.

(36) Some in Venezuela fear that the country may soon use up its oil reserves and plunge back into poverty. (37) Therefore, the government is slowing oil production and promoting other industries and natural resources. (38) Deposits of natural gas, iron ore, gold and diamonds, and fertile lands that produce coffee, cocoa, and sugar should guarantee Venezuela's prosperity for some time to come.

1. What did the explorers find in South America in the 1500s?

    Sentence   **(1)**   **(2)**   **(3)**   **(4)**   **(5)**

2. What shape does the perimeter of Venezuela form?

    Sentence   **(6)**   **(7)**   **(8)**   **(9)**   **(10)**

3. Besides Brazil, what country borders Venezuela on the east?

    Sentence   **(9)**   **(10)**   **(11)**   **(12)**   **(13)**

4. Has the history of Venezuela changed in recent years?

    Sentence   **(14)**   **(15)**   **(16)**   **(17)**   **(18)**

5. Until the 1800s, who settled and ruled the country?

    Sentence   **(16)**   **(17)**   **(18)**   **(19)**   **(20)**

6. Was the colony a wealthy one?

    Sentence   **(19)**   **(20)**   **(21)**   **(22)**   **(23)**

7. Among the countries of the world, how does Venezuela rank in exporting oil?

    Sentence   **(22)**   **(23)**   **(24)**   **(25)**   **(26)**

8. Do most of Venezuela's export earnings come from oil?

    Sentence   **(26)**   **(27)**   **(28)**   **(29)**   **(30)**

9. Have any oil wells been erected in Lake Maracaibo?

    Sentence   **(27)**   **(28)**   **(29)**   **(30)**   **(31)**

10. What is the *joropo*?

    Sentence   **(32)**   **(33)**   **(34)**   **(35)**   **(36)**

UNIT 17
Meat and Wheat

(1) Argentina is the second largest country in South America. (2) Only Brazil is larger. (3) Argentina stretches 2,300 miles from the tropics in the north to the southern tip on the windswept island of Tierra del Fuego, which Argentina shares with Chile. (4) The country extends over the greater part of southern South America and is the home of 31 million persons. (5) In area, Argentina is the eighth largest country in the world.

(6) Argentina is one of the great food-producing countries of the world. (7) A region called the Pampas provides ninety-five percent of the nation's corn. (8) Argentina, next to China and Brazil, is the world's third leading grower of corn. (9) Wheat occupies an even greater number of acres. (10) It is the nation's leading crop and accounts for eighty percent of all the wheat grown on the continent.

(11) For many years the cattle industry was of little importance. (12) However, the fencing of ranges with barbed wire and the introduction of improved breeding stock from Europe contributed much to the growth of the industry. (13) Before the development of refrigeration, fresh beef could not be transported to foreign lands without spoiling. (14) With refrigerated packing plants and refrigerated ships, the industry has made remarkable growth.

(15) The country's exports reflect Argentina's overwhelming dependence on agricultural products. (16) Farm and livestock products account for ninety percent of Argentina's export earnings. (17) Although the nation exports huge quantities of beef, the people of the Argentine still consume more beef per person than any other people in the world.

(18) The official language of Argentina is Spanish. (19) Argentine Spanish, however, has developed many differences from the language spoken in Spain. (20) Because of the large immigration of Italians, Germans, French, and Swiss to the land, many foreign words and phrases have been added to the language. (21) The pronunciation of Spanish has also been affected by the influx of foreigners.

(22) Buenos Aires, Argentina's capital city, attracts tourists from all over South America and the rest of the world. (23) Its fashionable stores, splendid art galleries, and elegant restaurants make it the "Paris of South America." (24) The sophisticated city of nearly ten million people (including suburbs) offers a wide choice of activities found in few South American cities. (25) Sidewalk cafés, sports arenas, museums, modern apartment houses, and views of many magnificent mansions satisfy the most varied interests.

(26) Mar del Plata and Miramar, important ocean resorts near Buenos Aires, as well as the capital itself, attract many visitors. (27) Cordoba offers visitors contact with Argentina's rich colonial past through its old buildings and cathedrals. (28) Another attraction is the spectacular two-mile-wide Iguassú Falls. (29) These falls, made up of 275 separate waterfalls, offer an awe-inspiring view. (30) The falls, on the border of Argentina and Brazil, are now part of a national park. (31) "We have more than beef," Argentineans say. "There's beauty too." (32) Those who visit the land say, "Si."

UNIT 17
Meat and Wheat

1. What is the largest country in South America?

    Sentence   **(1)**   **(2)**   **(3)**   **(4)**   **(5)**

2. What region provides most of the nation's corn?

    Sentence   **(4)**   **(5)**   **(6)**   **(7)**   **(8)**

3. Was the cattle industry always important?

    Sentence   **(7)**   **(8)**   **(9)**   **(10)**   **(11)**

4. What kind of fences are found on the ranges?

    Sentence   **(10)**   **(11)**   **(12)**   **(13)**   **(14)**

5. Do Americans consume more beef than Argentineans?

    Sentence   **(13)**   **(14)**   **(15)**   **(16)**   **(17)**

6. What is the official language of Argentina?

    Sentence   **(16)**   **(17)**   **(18)**   **(19)**   **(20)**

7. The immigration of which peoples has resulted in new words being added to the language?

    Sentence   **(19)**   **(20)**   **(21)**   **(22)**   **(23)**

8. How many people live in the Buenos Aires area?

    Sentence   **(22)**   **(23)**   **(24)**   **(25)**   **(26)**

9. Which city spotlights the historical aspect?

    Sentence   **(25)**   **(26)**   **(27)**   **(28)**   **(29)**

10. Where are the Iguassú Falls found?

    Sentence   **(28)**   **(29)**   **(30)**   **(31)**   **(32)**

(1) Scotland, slightly smaller than our state of Maine, occupies the northern third of Great Britain. (2) Ireland lies to the southwest across the narrow North Channel. (3) England is located to the south. (4) To the north and northwest lies the Atlantic Ocean. (5) To the east, across the North Sea, are the Scandinavian countries. (6) Because of the warming influences of the Gulf Stream, which churns by its coast, Scotland has a mild climate for a place so far north. (7) It is divided by geographical features into three distinct regions.

(8) The northernmost region of Scotland is the Highlands. (9) This area is wild and beautiful. (10) Covered by rugged mountains, it is often swept by fierce winds and driving rain. (11) This sparsely populated area has great tracts of uninhabited moors. (12) Highlanders engage in fishing and in farming small patches of land. (13) The western coastal region resembles that of Norway with its numerous narrow inlets framed by great cliffs. (14) Nowhere in Scotland is it possible to travel more than fifty miles without coming upon salt water.

(15) The Central Lowlands, lying between the Highlands and the Southern Uplands, contain Scotland's finest farmland. (16) The Central Lowlands stretch in a narrow belt across the "waist" of the country. (17) In this area is Scotland's most famed city, Edinburgh, its capital and oldest urban center. (18) The area is famed not only for its agriculture but also for its industry, especially shipbuilding.

(19) The Southern Uplands are the region nearest to England. (20) The inhabitants of this area are much like the people of northern England. (21) They speak English with a Scottish dialect, which often makes their English difficult for outsiders to understand. (22) The mild, damp climate of this area favors stock raising. (23) Cattle are grazed in the lower sections and sheep in the uplands. (24) Mutton and milk are the leading farm products.

(25) Scotland's agricultural areas are mostly limited to bottom lands. (26) Soil erosion has had a damaging effect on the ground cover. (27) Because of heavy rains, overgrazing, and steep terrain, the soil has settled into the valleys or has been washed out to sea. (28) Narrow plains and fertile valleys mark the places where farming can be carried on with adequate yields.

(29) Long ago the rugged land of Scotland caused its people to be separated into groups called "clans." (30) Each group had its own chief and its own tartan. (31) A tartan is a woolen material with a plaid design. (32) Although kilts, bagpipes, and clans may have originated only with the Highlanders, today they are the symbols of all Scotland.

(33) Scotland is a delight to tourists. (34) Visitors, particularly from the United States and British Commonwealth countries, enjoy the haunting beauty of its windswept mountains, its ruins of ancient castles, its bright green pastures, and its sparkling blue lakes. (35) Rare is the traveler who can resist the spell of bonnie (pleasant, excellent) Scotland.

UNIT 18
A Bonnie Land

1. What country is south of Scotland?
   Sentence   **(1)**   **(2)**   **(3)**   **(4)**   **(5)**

2. Why is the climate of Scotland mild?
   Sentence   **(4)**   **(5)**   **(6)**   **(7)**   **(8)**

3. Into how many regions is Scotland divided?
   Sentence   **(7)**   **(8)**   **(9)**   **(10)**   **(11)**

4. Is western Scotland similar to another land?
   Sentence   **(11)**   **(12)**   **(13)**   **(14)**   **(15)**

5. Is more than one major occupation carried on in the Central Lowlands?
   Sentence   **(15)**   **(16)**   **(17)**   **(18)**   **(19)**

6. What area is closest to England?
   Sentence   **(18)**   **(19)**   **(20)**   **(21)**   **(22)**

7. Is the climate favorable for stock raising?
   Sentence   **(21)**   **(22)**   **(23)**   **(24)**   **(25)**

8. What are Scotland's leading farm products?
   Sentence   **(24)**   **(25)**   **(26)**   **(27)**   **(28)**

9. How does the author describe a tartan?
   Sentence   **(28)**   **(29)**   **(30)**   **(31)**   **(32)**

10. What are some of the things that tourists like about Scotland?
    Sentence   **(31)**   **(32)**   **(33)**   **(34)**   **(35)**

(**1**) Austria is a storybook land. (**2**) Soaring mountains, castles perched high above rushing rivers, green forests, and mirrorlike lakes cast a spell of enchantment on the visitor. (**3**) So do its people, with their lighthearted spirit and customs.

(**4**) Few other lands in Europe have as many mountains as this nation. (**5**) Three-fourths of the country is covered by the Alps. (**6**) About thirty-seven percent of the land is carpeted with forests of spruce, larch, and beech. (**7**) Austria is one of the few countries in Europe that export lumber. (**8**) Tar, pitch, and turpentine also supply foreign markets.

(**9**) Rushing mountain streams have led Austrians to develop hydroelectric power resources. (**10**) However, this power is controversial, and the country imports much energy. (**11**) Austria also produces crude oil, ranking third in Europe.

(**12**) Before World War I, Austria was a far larger country than it is now, with a line of emperors dating back to the thirteenth century. (**13**) Even the loss of this empire in that war and the destruction suffered during World War II have not affected the people and their way of life. (**14**) "Bend, but don't break," is the advice they give.

(**15**) Such an attitude makes itself felt in many ways. (**16**) The cheeriness of Viennese waltzes has set the world to dancing. (**17**) Austrians' love for life can be found also in their fondness for food. (**18**) Eating is a favorite pastime, especially if the meal includes sweets and pastries.

(**19**) Over one-fifth of the nation's $7\frac{1}{2}$ million people live in the capital city, Vienna. (**20**) The city is famous for its theaters, for its art galleries, and, above all, for its music. (**21**) The Vienna Boys' Choir, for example, dates back to 1498. (**22**) Both Bach and Beethoven enjoyed the city so much that they spent much of their lives there. (**23**) Austria has produced many famous musicians of its own, including Mozart; Schubert; Haydn; and the "waltz kings," Johann Strauss, father and son. (**24**) It is rumored that Vienna is the only city in the world where musicians can pick up the telephone and ask for a perfect "A" note with which to tune their instruments!

(**25**) In medical science Austria has played a leading role. (**26**) There has been a college of medicine in Austria since 1365—over a hundred years before Columbus discovered America! (**27**) This place of learning is the world-renowned Vienna School of Medicine. (**28**) Austria produced Sigmund Freud, the father of psychiatry. (**29**) Austrian-born scientists have won five Nobel Prizes in medicine.

(**30**) Austria's economy is chiefly industrial. (**31**) Fewer than one out of every five persons earns a living from agriculture or forestry. (**32**) Yet Austria produces over three-fourths of its own foodstuffs. (**33**) Mining and heavy industry are major parts of the economy. (**34**) The Austrians have also won a reputation for being fine machinists. (**35**) The ship's propeller is among many Austrian inventions.

(**36**) Austrians are fond of outdoor sports. (**37**) The country is only as big as South Carolina, but it contains hundreds of skating rinks and two thousand ski lifts. (**38**) No other nation has won as many gold medals in Alpine ski events in the Olympic Games.

1. What kind of people are the Austrians?

    Sentence   **(1)**   **(2)**   **(3)**   **(4)**   **(5)**

2. What percentage of Austria is covered by forests?

    Sentence   **(5)**   **(6)**   **(7)**   **(8)**   **(9)**

3. What kind of power do streams provide?

    Sentence   **(9)**   **(10)**   **(11)**   **(12)**   **(13)**

4. What expression tells us the Austrian attitude toward misfortune?

    Sentence   **(13)**   **(14)**   **(15)**   **(16)**   **(17)**

5. Where do more than one-fifth of the people live?

    Sentence   **(17)**   **(18)**   **(19)**   **(20)**   **(21)**

6. Did any musicians of the past enjoy Vienna?

    Sentence   **(21)**   **(22)**   **(23)**   **(24)**   **(25)**

7. Was Freud the only Austrian to get recognition for his work in medicine?

    Sentence   **(25)**   **(26)**   **(27)**   **(28)**   **(29)**

8. Does Austria have an industrial economy?

    Sentence   **(26)**   **(27)**   **(28)**   **(29)**   **(30)**

9. How many people earn a living from agriculture?

    Sentence   **(31)**   **(32)**   **(33)**   **(34)**   **(35)**

10. In what sport have Austrians excelled?

    Sentence   **(34)**   **(35)**   **(36)**   **(37)**   **(38)**

A. Exercising Your Skill

In Units 13 through 19, you read about the countries of Japan, Chile, Korea, Venezuela, Argentina, Scotland, and Austria. In your reading, you have come across dates that mark important events in some of these countries' histories. Information about dates and events can often be found on time lines. A time line summarizes or organizes information. Below is a sample time line covering the twenty-five year period from 1800 to 1825. It shows important events in South American independence.

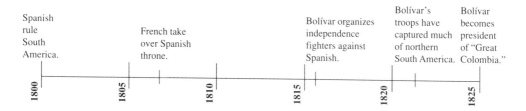

You have probably seen many time lines in your social studies or history books. Think about what you know about time lines, and look at the sample above. Read the phrases below. Decide which ones relate to time lines. On your paper, write the heading <u>Time Lines</u>. Under it, write the phrases you chose.

- give dates of important events
- name important events
- tell order of events
- explain outcome of events
- show amount of time between events
- tell which events on the line are more important than the others

B. Expanding Your Skill

Read the following paragraph about Spanish conquests in the Americas. On your paper, summarize the dated information on a time line like the one below.

Columbus reached the shores of the Americas in 1492. After that, Spanish explorers, in their quest for gold, captured lands from the native inhabitants. Cortés conquered the Aztecs in Mexico in 1521. In 1532 Pizarro overthrew the great Incan empire in Peru. Hernando de Soto traveled into North America, exploring the area around the Mississippi River in 1541. Francisco de Coronado conquered the Zuni pueblo people in 1540. In 1560, Spain claimed many of these lands in North America as "New Mexico."

C. Exploring Language

The time line below summarizes events in the early British settlement of North America. Use information on the time line to write a three-paragraph report about this time period. Use social studies, history, or library books to gather more details for the paragraphs. You may want to use the outline below to organize your material.

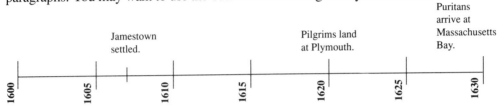

I. Jamestown Settled
   A. (reasons for settlement)
   B. (settlers)
   C. (first year)
   D. (leader or leaders)

II. Plymouth Settled
   A. (reasons for settlement)
   B. (settlers)
   C. (first year)
   D. (leader or leaders)

III. Massachusetts Bay Colony Settled
   A. (reasons for settlement)
   B. (settlers)
   C. (first year)
   D. (leader or leaders)

D. Expressing Yourself

Choose one of these activities.

1. On a piece of paper, write a time line of your life like the one below. Begin with the year of your birth. On the line, mark off and label the dates of other events you consider important in your life. You can continue this project over time.

2. With other classmates, create a school-year time line. Talk about which of the year's events are most important. Mark off and label these important events. Begin the time line with the first month of the school year, and end it with the last month of the school year.

UNIT 20
Land of Culture

(1) "Every man has two countries, his own and France," wrote President Thomas Jefferson. (2) The President had a unique way of saying that France had given the world so much that is fine and beautiful that people everywhere had come to love it. (3) It was his way of acknowledging France's cultural inspiration to the world, one that has continued for more than a thousand years.

(4) Because the French have held such a prominent place in the field of arts and sciences for so many centuries, they are often called the most civilized people on earth. (5) Many of the world's most famous artists, writers, sculptors, and scientists have been French.

(6) The list of France's immortals is a listing of some of the world's outstanding figures. (7) Among musical composers, Ravel, Gounod, and Debussy occupy a high position. (8) Sculptor Rodin ranks among the immortals with his stone and bronze creations. (9) Proust, Balzac, and Voltaire are appreciated in whatever language their words are translated. (10) Braille and Pasteur were scientists whose fame extends far beyond the borders of their native land. (11) Corot, Monet, Cézanne, and Matisse are but a few of the galaxy of talented French artists.

(12) The skills of the French have been not only intellectual but also practical. (13) French crafts produce countless beautiful objects. (14) Fine lace, handbags, jewelry, carpets, and other products continue to maintain France's reputation for careful artisanship. (15) In addition to the goods made by hand or in small shops, the French, in their factories, produce modern cars, chemicals, watches, glassware, and textiles.

(16) One-tenth of the French working force is engaged in agriculture. (17) While most farms are small (about thirty-seven acres on the average), France's farm products meet national needs and still allow a remainder for export. (18) Sugar beets are important. (19) A part of the farmers' income stems from livestock. (20) Vast fields of flowers are grown for the oils that are extracted and used in perfumes and soaps.

(21) Fruit is a French specialty. (22) One particular fruit, the grape, is of special importance to French farmers. (23) Over four million acres are devoted to this crop. (24) Nearly every farmer cultivates at least a few acres. (25) From the grapes the French make high-quality wine and export it worldwide. (26) Almost two billion gallons of wine are produced annually.

(27) Tourists who journey to France almost always visit Paris. (28) Known as the "City of Light," Paris is one of the world's most beautiful cities. (29) It is like no other. (30) It lies open to the sky. (31) No shadows from tall buildings darken its streets. (32) Tree-lined boulevards, shady parks, and outdoor restaurants give Paris an atmosphere all its own. (33) Graceful monuments, museums, and art galleries are all reminders of the cultural tradition that belongs to France.

UNIT 20
Land of Culture

1. For how long has France provided inspiration in the field of culture?
   Sentence   **(1)**   **(2)**   **(3)**   **(4)**   **(5)**

2. Why are the French said to be the most civilized people?
   Sentence   **(4)**   **(5)**   **(6)**   **(7)**   **(8)**

3. Who were some famous French authors?
   Sentence   **(7)**   **(8)**   **(9)**   **(10)**   **(11)**

4. Does France have a reputation for careful artisanship?
   Sentence   **(10)**   **(11)**   **(12)**   **(13)**   **(14)**

5. Is France self-sufficient in food production?
   Sentence   **(13)**   **(14)**   **(15)**   **(16)**   **(17)**

6. Why do the farmers raise flowers?
   Sentence   **(16)**   **(17)**   **(18)**   **(19)**   **(20)**

7. What fruit is of special importance?
   Sentence   **(18)**   **(19)**   **(20)**   **(21)**   **(22)**

8. How do we know that other people enjoy French wine?
   Sentence   **(21)**   **(22)**   **(23)**   **(24)**   **(25)**

9. What is Paris' nickname?
   Sentence   **(26)**   **(27)**   **(28)**   **(29)**   **(30)**

10. What are some reminders of the cultural tradition?
    Sentence **(29)**   **(30)**   **(31)**   **(32)**   **(33)**

UNIT 21
Land of Treasures

(1) Narrow, boot-shaped Italy extends into the Mediterranean Sea almost to the coast of Africa. (2) The nation includes the major islands of Sicily and Sardinia. (3) Sicily lies off the toe of the Italian boot and looks as if it is about to be kicked across the Mediterranean. (4) Sardinia is about one hundred miles northwest of Sicily. (5) Italy is more than one-third covered by mountains, including the mighty Alps, which separate it from its European neighbors.

(6) It is the mountainous character of the land that makes farming so difficult in Italy. (7) Added drawbacks of poor soil and inadequate rainfall compel Italian farmers to work with marvelous skill in their attempt to grow enough food for the crowded land. (8) Cereals, grown in the north, are Italy's most important crops. (9) Despite the success of agriculture, Italy must import foodstuffs to meet the needs of its people.

(10) Northern Italy is the industrial as well as the leading agricultural region. (11) It is in the north that the metal industry has shown such a phenomenal growth. (12) Sewing machines, typewriters, adding machines, machine tools, and attractive Italian automobiles are produced there.

(13) It is also in the north that the textile industry is centered. (14) Italy today is one of the world's fashion centers. (15) Shoes, belts, handbags, ties, shirts, and similar products possess the style that makes them sought after all over the world. (16) With these profitable exports, superb Italian workers have overcome the nation's severe lack of raw materials.

(17) Many of the greatest names in the history of Western culture have been Italian. (18) In the fields of art, literature, and music, many rank among the immortals. (19) Artists Leonardo da Vinci and Raphael have left the world art treasures that are priceless. (20) One of the great sculptors of all ages, Michelangelo, was born in the little town of Caprese, near Florence. (21) His statue of David is considered one of the finest works of art in existence. (22) Italy's greatest writer was Dante. (23) His classical poems are among the finest written in any language. (24) Verdi and Puccini composed noted operas. (25) It was the Italian, Stradivari, who made the finest violins in history. (26) Those fond of music know the names Enrico Caruso, Arturo Toscanini, Renata Tebaldi, Licia Albanese, and Renata Scotto.

(27) In the fields of science, inventions, and discoveries, Italians have also won fame. (28) Scientists Galileo, Volta, Marconi, and Fermi are possibly the best known. (29) Explorers Cabot, Columbus, Verrazano, and Vespucci ranged far from home to discover new lands to the west.

(30) Sunny Italy, known for its beautiful scenery and art treasures, attracts an ever-increasing flow of tourists. (31) Many stop at Pisa to see its Leaning Tower. (32) Others are drawn to Venice, a city that rests gracefully on mud banks crisscrossed by pretty canals. (33) The city of Florence is a mecca to those who value art. (34) Rome, the Eternal City, with its galleries, ancient buildings, and museums, is the goal of all who visit the "Land of Treasures."

1. Where is Sicily located?

   Sentence   **(1)**   **(2)**   **(3)**   **(4)**   **(5)**

2. How is Italy separated from its neighbors?

   Sentence   **(4)**   **(5)**   **(6)**   **(7)**   **(8)**

3. Is Italy self-sufficient in food?

   Sentence   **(7)**   **(8)**   **(9)**   **(10)**   **(11)**

4. Is Northern Italy an industrial region?

   Sentence   **(10)**   **(11)**   **(12)**   **(13)**   **(14)**

5. Is the textile industry centered in the North?

   Sentence   **(13)**   **(14)**   **(15)**   **(16)**   **(17)**

6. Does Italy have a lack of raw materials?

   Sentence   **(16)**   **(17)**   **(18)**   **(19)**   **(20)**

7. In what fields of culture have Italians achieved rare distinction?

   Sentence   **(18)**   **(19)**   **(20)**   **(21)**   **(22)**

8. Who was Italy's most talented writer?

   Sentence   **(22)**   **(23)**   **(24)**   **(25)**   **(26)**

9. In which direction did Italy's explorers discover new lands?

   Sentence   **(26)**   **(27)**   **(28)**   **(29)**   **(30)**

10. Where is the Leaning Tower located?

    Sentence   **(30)**   **(31)**   **(32)**   **(33)**   **(34)**

UNIT 22
The Land of Contrasts

(1) Spain, more than any land in Europe, is a "Land of Contrasts." (2) It is a mixture of the old and the new. (3) While possessing some of the oldest trains in Europe, Spain also has some of the most modern. (4) A train trip across Spain vividly illustrates the contrasts with which the country abounds. (5) A glance out of the train window at one time reveals fertile vineyards, at another time hardly a sign of plant life. (6) Modern cars are seen on the same roads as plodding oxen and burros. (7) Majestic castles and homes of rare elegance contrast with huts that shelter the extremely poor.

(8) The contrasts make Spain an exciting place to visit, and tourism has become a major industry. (9) Once seldom visited, Spain is now among the most popular of tourist lands. (10) Spain is also one of the least expensive countries to visit in all Europe. (11) Fifty million outsiders, mostly from western Europe and America, visit Spain annually. (12) Madrid, the capital, and Andalusia, in the sunny south, are areas most frequented by tourists.

(13) Visitors to Madrid are almost certain to tour the Prado Museum. (14) It houses one of the finest collections of art in the world. (15) In this museum the works of Louisa Roldon, Velasquez, Ribera, Murillo, Goya, and El Greco are on display. (16) Greek-born El Greco is considered a Spanish painter because most of his outstanding work was done in Spain. (17) Besides the old masters, Spain's modern-day painters Salvador Dali and Pablo Picasso are known throughout the world.

(18) A person who had visited Spain around 1950 would see another startling contrast on returning today. (19) Up to the 1950s agriculture was Spain's main source of income, and half of its population worked on farms. (20) But industry has grown amazingly since then; industrial income is now $2\frac{1}{2}$ times as great as farm income. (21) Spain is now one of the world's leaders in manufacturing ships and cars. (22) Millions of its people are climbing out of poverty through industrial jobs.

(23) Most of the people speak Castilian Spanish, the official language based on the dialect of Castile. (24) Although it comes mainly from Latin, it contains quite a number of words from Arabic, the language of the Moors, African invaders who occupied Spain for seven hundred years. (25) Castilian Spanish is taught in the schools and is spoken by all of the educated. (26) Native dialects are spoken in some regions, principally in Galicia, Catalonia, and the Basque provinces.

(27) Spain was once the mightiest nation on earth. (28) The country reached its peak in the 1500s. (29) Treasure galleons came into Spanish ports carrying gold and silver from its colonies in Latin America. (30) The riches, however, were exhausted in a long series of wars. (31) One by one, Spain lost its colonies, and today a formerly great overseas empire consists of only a few areas in Africa. (32) The country has known periods of prosperity and periods of poverty. (33) Even in its history and its rank among nations, Spain is a "Land of Contrasts."

UNIT 22
The Land of Contrasts

1. In what general way is Spain a "Land of Contrasts"?

   Sentence   **(1)**   **(2)**   **(3)**   **(4)**   **(5)**

2. Why has Spain been so popular among tourists?

   Sentence   **(4)**   **(5)**   **(6)**   **(7)**   **(8)**

3. What is another reason why many people visit Spain?

   Sentence   **(7)**   **(8)**   **(9)**   **(10)**   **(11)**

4. How many outsiders visit Spain each year?

   Sentence   **(11)**   **(12)**   **(13)**   **(14)**   **(15)**

5. Did Spain have any modern-day painters of merit?

   Sentence   **(14)**   **(15)**   **(16)**   **(17)**   **(18)**

6. What percentage of the population worked on farms before the 1950s?

   Sentence   **(17)**   **(18)**   **(19)**   **(20)**   **(21)**

7. Is Castilian Spanish spoken?

   Sentence   **(20)**   **(21)**   **(22)**   **(23)**   **(24)**

8. In which regions are native dialects still spoken?

   Sentence   **(23)**   **(24)**   **(25)**   **(26)**   **(27)**

9. When was Spain all-powerful?

   Sentence   **(26)**   **(27)**   **(28)**   **(29)**   **(30)**

10. Has Spain kept all its colonies?

    Sentence   **(29)**   **(30)**   **(31)**   **(32)**   **(33)**

UNIT 23
Switzerland of Africa

(1) Ethiopia, a source of the Nile River, is one of the oldest kingdoms in all of Africa. (2) Only Egypt is more ancient. (3) Ethiopia's independence traces back to 1000 B.C., though little was known about the country until relatively modern times. (4) Early Greek and Roman writers called it the "Land Beyond the Sunrise." (5) They often referred to Ethiopia's wealth and power.

(6) The shape of Ethiopia is roughly that of a triangle with its point facing north. (7) The nation's long, northern coastline lies on the Red Sea. (8) Ethiopia was land-locked until 1962, when Eritrea became part of the country. (9) The Territory of Afars and Issus and the Somali Republic lie to the east, Kenya to the south, and Sudan to the west. (10) Most of Ethiopia lies on a plateau that stands above the surrounding desert lowland.

(11) Many of the animals associated with Africa are found in Ethiopia. (12) Monkeys abound in many regions. (13) The elephant and the rhinoceros are widespread. (14) Hippopotamuses and crocodiles inhabit lakes and rivers. (15) Snakes, including pythons and cobras, are common. (16) Lions are occasionally encountered in the southern part of the country. (17) Leopards found there are unusually large. (18) Fierce hyenas are found everywhere, even in the nation's capital city!

(19) Addis Ababa, the capital and largest city, lies eight thousand feet above sea level. (20) The city has a population of almost $1\frac{1}{4}$ million. (21) Its name means "New Flower." (22) The high elevation of the city gives it a cool climate. (23) Modern build-ings, hospitals, libraries, a museum, and a university impress visitors. (24) Three miles from the city a modern airfield links Ethiopia with Europe and neighboring African countries.

(25) Since the early 1970s Ethiopia has been suffering from famine. (26) More than ninety percent of the labor force is engaged in agriculture, so the famine hit the country very hard. (27) Vegetable and grain supplies disappeared. (28) Huge numbers of cattle and sheep could not be fed. (29) A worldwide relief effort began in 1984. (30) Other nations sent food, money, and workers to help Ethiopians overcome the famine.

(31) Ethiopia's most important crop has always been coffee. (32) Ethiopians are skilled coffee farmers. (33) Almost all the coffee is grown at altitudes between four thousand and seven thousand feet. (34) Ethiopia is generally regarded as the original home of the coffee tree. (35) The word *coffee* comes from the Kaffa region of the southwestern part of the country. (36) The curbing of soil erosion and the increased use of fertilizers and irrigation could radically increase crop production.

(37) Ethiopia is making an effort to improve both the health and the education of its people. (38) Progress is being made in recovering from famine. (39) However, to insure against famine in the future, more is needed. (40) Farm experts say that modern techniques must be established in order for Ethiopians to farm successfully. (41) With the continued help of worldwide aid, Ethiopians are working to preserve life and beau-ty in "The Switzerland of Africa."

UNIT 23
Switzerland of Africa

1. Does the Nile have a source in Ethiopia?
   Sentence   **(1)**   **(2)**   **(3)**   **(4)**   **(5)**

2. What is the shape of Ethiopia?
   Sentence   **(5)**   **(6)**   **(7)**   **(8)**   **(9)**

3. Is Kenya to the south of Ethiopia?
   Sentence   **(8)**   **(9)**   **(10)**   **(11)**   **(12)**

4. Are there many monkeys in Ethiopia?
   Sentence   **(11)**   **(12)**   **(13)**   **(14)**   **(15)**

5. Where would a person not expect to find wild animals?
   Sentence   **(16)**   **(17)**   **(18)**   **(19)**   **(20)**

6. What has been happening in Ethiopia since the early 1970s?
   Sentence   **(22)**   **(23)**   **(24)**   **(25)**   **(26)**

7. Which animals could not be fed?
   Sentence   **(25)**   **(26)**   **(27)**   **(28)**   **(29)**

8. What is the most important crop?
   Sentence   **(31)**   **(32)**   **(33)**   **(34)**   **(35)**

9. In what ways could Ethiopia improve its coffee production?
   Sentence   **(34)**   **(35)**   **(36)**   **(37)**   **(38)**

10. Do Ethiopian farmers need modern techniques?
    Sentence   **(36)**   **(37)**   **(38)**   **(39)**   **(40)**

UNIT 24
Lively Land Below the Border

(1) Just south of the United States lies the land of Mexico. (2) It is shaped like a horn. (3) The top of the horn borders on the United States for two thousand miles. (4) The southern and narrower end borders on two Central American countries, Guatemala and Belize. (5) On the east are the Gulf of Mexico and the Caribbean Sea. (6) To the west are the Gulf of California and the Pacific Ocean. (7) Mexico is not a small country. (8) If it were placed on the continent of Europe, it would extend across Germany, Austria, and Italy.

(9) Few countries match Mexico in scenery. (10) Towering mountains, grim deserts, and steaming jungles are all found in this Latin American republic. (11) Though the terrain and elevation provide for a variety of crops, these same features limit the number of acres that can be farmed. (12) Only about one acre in eight of the total land area is fit for farming. (13) In places where the soil is fertile, insufficient rain has stood in the way of agricultural growth.

(14) These serious disadvantages are being overcome. (15) The government has built huge irrigation projects to make dry land fertile. (16) It has also modernized transportation to markets. (17) Many farmers are learning to use new, improved fertilizers, seeds, and varieties of crops. (18) Corn is the nation's leading crop. (19) Next come beans, wheat, cotton, sugar cane, and coffee. (20) Beans and corn make up the main part of a Mexican's diet. (21) Despite Mexico's overall agricultural progress, thousands of small farms, called *ejidos*, yield so little as to keep those who work on them in poverty.

(22) Mexico has rich mineral deposits. (23) Most of these deposits are in the Sierra Madre range. (24) Mexico is a leading producer of silver. (25) The country ranks high in the production of sulphur, lead, zinc, and gold also. (26) Today Mexico's most valuable mineral resource is its vast petroleum deposits.

(27) Mexico City is the nation's capital and the center for industry and culture. (28) Monuments, fountains, wide avenues, modern apartment buildings, and old colonial-style Spanish cathedrals make the city among the most attractive in the hemisphere. (29) Like the entire country, Mexico City is growing rapidly. (30) The city and its suburbs make up the world's most heavily populated metropolitan area, with over fifteen million people!

(31) Mexico is an active world trader. (32) Valuable oil has become its principal export. (33) Mexico is one of the five largest oil producers in the world. (34) Zinc, lead, and copper are other mineral exports. (35) From its fields and waters Mexico ships cotton, sugar, coffee, and shrimp around the world. (36) Mexico imports mostly food, machinery, and manufactured goods.

(37) Tourists are "big business" in Mexico. (38) Many come to visit the ruins of the ancient Aztec and Mayan civilizations. (39) Others journey to Acapulco on Mexico's west coast for relaxation on its splendid beaches. (40) Still others come to observe Mexico's arts, handicrafts, and fiestas. (41) For whatever reason, tourists arrive in great numbers, over five million a year. (42) They spend over a billion dollars.

UNIT 24
Lively Land Below the Border

1. What is the length of Mexico's border with the United States?

   Sentence (1) (2) (3) (4) (5)

2. What kind of scenery is found in Mexico?

   Sentence (6) (7) (8) (9) (10)

3. What factors other than rainfall limit the land area suitable for farming?

   Sentence (8) (9) (10) (11) (12)

4. Has insufficient rain stood in the way of agriculture?

   Sentence (11) (12) (13) (14) (15)

5. What are other leading crops grown besides corn?

   Sentence (15) (16) (17) (18) (19)

6. Does Mexico have rich mineral deposits?

   Sentence (18) (19) (20) (21) (22)

7. Where are most of the deposits found?

   Sentence (23) (24) (25) (26) (27)

8. What makes Mexico City so attractive?

   Sentence (28) (29) (30) (31) (32)

9. What are the leading imports?

   Sentence (33) (34) (35) (36) (37)

10. Why do tourists visit Acapulco?

    Sentence (38) (39) (40) (41) (42)

UNIT 25
Birthplace of Civilization

(1) It is difficult to overestimate the importance of Greece in the history of civilization. (2) Its influence on the rest of the world has been immense. (3) The ancient Greeks made discoveries in thought, art, architecture, government, and science that have shaped Western ideas ever since. (4) Our laws and culture are still based on Greek models.

(5) Greece, a nation to which other countries have every reason to be grateful, is a small country. (6) The land reaches down into the Mediterranean Sea. (7) Its many jagged peninsulas and islands suggest spread-out fingers touching the sea. (8) About four-fifths of the country is mountainous. (9) About a fifth of the land is composed of several hundred islands in the neighboring Aegean and Ionian seas.

(10) Although agriculture employs almost thirty percent of the labor force, less than one-third of the land is able to be farmed. (11) Wherever there is a patch of soil, however thin or stony, it must be plowed. (12) Olive trees and vineyards grow on much of the farmed land. (13) On the rugged hills farmers raise herds of sheep and goats.

(14) More than half of Greece is surrounded by water, and few places in the country are more than fifty miles from the sea. (15) Understandably, Greece became a seafaring nation early in its history. (16) Today Greece has merchant marine ships numbering over 2,600. (17) Merchant ships from other countries employ Greek crews. (18) This is important to the Greeks, as the nation has too many people for the jobs available in the homeland.

(19) In recent years tourism has made rapid gains. (20) The ruins of ancient Greece are the chief attraction for most visitors. (21) Perhaps the most popular ruin is the Parthenon in Athens. (22) It is located atop a hill called the Acropolis. (23) Although it is over two thousand years old, many architects still consider it the most beautiful building in the world.

(24) Most of us do not realize that each day we use words from the Greek language. (25) Words such as *athlete*, *plastic*, *music*, and *philosophy* are Greek in origin. (26) When we create new words, we often build them out of Greek words. (27) The word *philosophy* comes from the Greek *philein,* meaning "to love," and *sophia*, meaning "wisdom." (28) Thus *philosopher* originally meant "a lover of wisdom."

(29) It is fitting that the word *philosopher* came from the Greek language. (30) So many of the world's outstanding names in this field were of Greek birth. (31) Socrates, one of the great figures in the history of thought, was born in Athens. (32) He guided people to search for the truth. (33) Plato and Aristotle are other Greek immortals who inspired students to search for truth and knowledge. (34) While they devoted themselves to people's minds, Hippocrates devoted his life to the care of bodies. (35) He is known today as the "Father of Medicine." (36) The great gift of Greece has been the inspiration it has provided the world for improving both the mind and the body.

UNIT 25
Birthplace of Civilization

1. Is Greece a small country?

   Sentence   **(1)**   **(2)**   **(3)**   **(4)**   **(5)**

2. Is the Greek coast irregular in its outline?

   Sentence   **(4)**   **(5)**   **(6)**   **(7)**   **(8)**

3. What percentage of the land is mountainous?

   Sentence   **(7)**   **(8)**   **(9)**   **(10)**   **(11)**

4. What land is suitable for raising sheep?

   Sentence   **(11)**   **(12)**   **(13)**   **(14)**   **(15)**

5. Is it easy to find employment in Greece?

   Sentence   **(14)**   **(15)**   **(16)**   **(17)**   **(18)**

6. In what activity have there been important gains?

   Sentence   **(18)**   **(19)**   **(20)**   **(21)**   **(22)**

7. What is probably the most popular ruin in Athens?

   Sentence   **(21)**   **(22)**   **(23)**   **(24)**   **(25)**

8. What do most of us use from the Greek language?

   Sentence   **(24)**   **(25)**   **(26)**   **(27)**   **(28)**

9. What does *sophia* mean?

   Sentence   **(27)**   **(28)**   **(29)**   **(30)**   **(31)**

10. How did Socrates help people?

    Sentence   **(32)**   **(33)**   **(34)**   **(35)**   **(36)**

The Last L A P
Language Activity Pages

In Units 20 through 25, you read about the countries of France, Italy, Spain, Ethiopia, Mexico, and Greece. People who travel to countries such as these often go by airplane. Once in a country, they often find it convenient to travel by bus or train.

A. Exercising Your Skill

Schedules, or timetables, help people find out when planes, buses, or trains arrive or depart. Schedules are arranged in rows and columns, like charts. With a partner, talk about the types of information that appear on schedules. Make up a sample schedule to show how the information could be arranged. You may want to use the following form as a guide to get started.

Train Number	Place A (depart)	Place B (arrive/depart)	Place C (arrive)

B. Expanding Your Skill

Decide which of the words below might appear on a plane, bus, or train schedule. Write them on a word wheel on your paper. You may use the form shown below. Remember that a schedule is *not* an advertisement.

tickets	coach	glittering	number
delicious	gate	nonstop	terminal
arrival	sandy	express	breathtaking
departure	local	track	reservations

Schedules

C. Exploring Language

Study the bus schedule below. Then read the answers that follow. Decide which of the answers come from information on the schedule. Write the number of each of those answers on your paper. Then write a question for those answers.

Bus Number	Leave Hartington	Arrive Valleyview	Leave Valleyview	Arrive Gate City
12	7:55 A.M.	8:15 A.M.	8:20 A.M.	8:45 A.M.
16	8:05 A.M.	8:25 A.M.	8:30 A.M.	8:55 A.M.
18	*9:00 A.M.	----------	----------	9:45 A.M.
24	12:10 P.M.	12:30 P.M.	12:35 P.M.	1:00 P.M.
28	*4:00 P.M.	----------	----------	4:45 P.M.
	* no stops			

1. arrives at 8:25 A.M.
2. 59 passengers
3. 12:35 P.M. to 1:00 P.M.
4. nonstop afternoon trip
5. forty-five minutes
6. midnight and later
7. 7:55 A.M. or 8:05 A.M.
8. bus 30
9. just after noon
10. at 4:45 P.M.

D. Expressing Yourself

Choose one of these activities.

1. Look at an actual bus or train schedule. Plan a trip that will take two weeks. Include stops in three different towns. If possible, find out how much the trip will cost. Work with a partner. Check each other's plan.

2. Make up a schedule of what you do from the time you awaken to the time you go to sleep. It should show your "arrivals" and "departures" during an average day. Use your imagination.